IMAGES
of America

MANHEIM

This aerial view shows a good portion of the beautiful town of Manheim along with part of the farmlands that lovingly encase the town in green fertility. This view is looking toward the west. The intersection in the lower left corner is at South Main and Stiegel Streets. (Manheim Historical Society.)

April Lynn Gibble Downey

Copyright © 2021 by April Lynn Gibble Downey
ISBN 978-1-4671-0614-6

Published by Arcadia Publishing
Charleston, South Carolina

Printed in the United States of America

Library of Congress Control Number: 2020943895

For all general information, please contact Arcadia Publishing:
Telephone 843-853-2070
Fax 843-853-0044
E-mail sales@arcadiapublishing.com
For customer service and orders:
Toll-Free 1-888-313-2665

Visit us on the Internet at www.arcadiapublishing.com

*Dedicated to my sweet, strong, amazing children:
I love you to the end of the universe and back.*

Contents

ACKNOWLEDGMENTS

It was during my ancestry research that the idea for this book first came to me. I discovered my paternal Gibble-Kreiner ancestors go back in the Manheim area for about 300 years, and my maternal Kauffman-Stull ancestors go back in western and central Pennsylvania for about 200 to 300 years. Before then, my ancestors primarily came from southwestern Germany and northern Switzerland, along with a couple of folks from Ireland and Scotland.

This book was primarily constructed with the help of the Manheim Historical Society (MHS). The MHS was established in 1964 by Herman Hart, Eugene and Doris Hollinger, Mayor Herbert Obetz, John D. Kendig, J. David Young, Harry B. Shearer, George L. Heiges, and Loy C. Awkerman. Many of these people were notable Manheim historians. The members of the MHS care for numerous photo albums, historical documents, and a small museum and library inside of the Harry B. Shearer Heritage Center. They also own and tend to historical properties around Manheim.

Manheim's history is also preserved through the community members and business owners who have long been proud of their pasts. Records, photographs, and artifacts are well loved in the community. Two groups of people should be specifically recognized. The first group includes the compilers of MHS's extensive volume *Manheim Revisited 1700–2000*, which was instrumental in the creation of this book; they include Bea Kreiner, Colin Williams, John Blanck, Inda Graybill, Anne Myers, Dennis Ober, and Duane Ober. The second group consists of Miles and Elizabeth Keiffer and the Historic Manheim Preservation Foundation, Inc., which is maintained in memory of the Keiffers.

I would like to thank all those who have encouraged me while researching and writing this book, especially Lonnie, who always supports and believes in me. I would also like to thank Susan Williams, the current president of the MHS, who helped open the door, and Tina Nelson for her invaluable gift to this project.

Additionally, I wish to convey sincere appreciation to the multitude of volunteers, donators, and contributors to historical societies, genealogies, museums, and publications that keep history alive in the hearts and minds of people like me.

INTRODUCTION

The colony of Pennsylvania ("Penn's Woods") began with the intention of it being a utopia of religious freedom and tolerance when it was given to William Penn on March 4, 1681, by King Charles II of England. Penn called the 45,000 acres a "holy experiment." In 1701, Penn established the Charter of Privileges, which granted religious tolerance to all citizens of the new colony (however, only non-Catholic Christians could hold governmental offices and vote). Despite feeling that Native Americans lived in "primitive" ways, he saw them as spiritually equal and tried to live peacefully with them and bought their lands instead of taking them, as was the common practice of colonists. The prospect of religious freedom was alluring to many people living in tumultuous Europe, which routinely implemented religious persecution. The English Quakers were first to immigrate into the religious freedom of this new colony, followed by the Amish and Mennonites—both of which were Anabaptist sects and comprised the largest group of non–English-speaking immigrants before 1720. These groups of Christian sects differed in beliefs and lifestyle from the predominant forms of European Christianity at the time. The people in these sects are often called "plain folks," as members wear plain, simple clothing; women wear head coverings; and all members abstain from aspects of modern society such as military service and most technology. They also practice only adult baptisms, as they believe baptizing babies is inappropriate, since infants cannot choose the faith for themselves. Most of these people were German-speaking immigrants who came from Switzerland and areas along the Rhine River in Germany. Following the influx of German-speaking immigrants, the Protestant Scots-Irish also came and settled in Pennsylvania. In addition to the plain sects looking for a safe home to practice their unique forms of Christianity, more mainstream religious folk came over from the Evangelical churches of Germany as well, which included the Moravians and Lutherans. The town of Manheim was primarily built by Lutherans, but the surrounding countryside was populated with many Mennonites, Amish, and Dunkards, who moved into the agricultural frontier of Lancaster County (officially established as a county in 1729).

In 1771, Pastor Frederick Muhlenberg, who preached in Manheim, noted that there were controversies and disagreements between the plain sects of the countryside and the Lutherans in town. However, together, these groups of German-speaking immigrants created a culture that is referred to as the Pennsylvania Dutch, which continues to this day. The Pennsylvania Dutch culture is expressed through traditional German foods and strong ties to agriculture, folk art, and a country German accent that can still be heard even among native English speakers. Many of the plain sects still speak Pennsylvania Dutch (the Pennsylvania dialect of German) fluently and sometimes exclusively. The folk art of the region is distinctive with its simple yet colorful designs of tulips, vines, birds, people, and geometric patterns. These designs are often found within circles and are called "hexes," originally created to be a form of Christian magic. (Admittedly, this is somewhat of an oversimplification of a complex topic left for other books.)

The town borough of Manheim formed out of Rapho Township (chartered in 1741) and is wedged alongside Penn Township (chartered in 1846) in northwestern Lancaster County near the Lebanon County border. (Readers should note that Manheim Township is southeast of Manheim and is not on the border of the borough proper.) Rapho Township was established from land originally allotted to Donegal Township. Despite the large number of incoming German-speaking folks, Rapho Township was named after a town in County Donegal in Ireland—a testament to the influence of the Scots-Irish who pioneered into Lancaster County along the Chiques Creek (alternative spellings of the creek's name include Chickies or Chiquesalunga). Generally speaking, the Swiss-German immigrants tended to settle in the north end of the township, while the Scots-Irish settled in the south.

The story of Manheim's founding begins with a German immigrant named Henry William Stiegel (born Heinrich Wilhelm Stiegel). He came to Philadelphia from Cologne, Germany, in 1750, crossing the Atlantic on a ship named *Nancy*. After arriving in Pennsylvania, Stiegel went to work for Jacob Huber at Elizabeth Furnace, just outside of Warwick Township, and became an ironmaster. Huber named his furnace after his daughter Elizabeth, whom Stiegel eventually married. While at Elizabeth Furnace, Stiegel also began making glass and thus started his enduring legacy as one of the finest glassmakers in early US history. The style of glass he worked in, which imitated the glasswork being imported from Europe at the time, is called Stiegel-type glass. In 1758, Henry Stiegel, his friends and business partners Charles and Alexander Stedman, and John Barr purchased Elizabeth Furnace from Jacob Huber; however, shortly afterward, Barr left the partnership. After much success at Elizabeth Furnace, Stiegel bought Tulpehocken Forge and changed its name to Charming Forge. In 1760, he officially became a citizen of Great Britain while in the colony of Pennsylvania.

In 1762, the year Manheim was officially founded, Charles and Alexander Stedman bought the 729 acres of land that would become Manheim from Isaac Norris and his daughter Mary, who inherited the land from Isaac's wife, Sarah, who had received it from her grandfather James Logan, who received the land directly from William Penn. That same year, the Stedmans sold one third of the land to Henry Stiegel. This land was a natural meadow with limited forests, and farmers used it to harvest hay for their livestock. Rapho Township, despite its Irish name, was overwhelmingly German-speaking in population, and so Stiegel and Stedman's new town was named after Mannheim, Germany, a town along the Rhine River in the German Palatinate where so many Pennsylvania immigrants came from. In addition to Charles and Alexander Stedman and Henry Stiegel, their wives—Ann, Elizabeth, and Elizabeth, respectively—were also on the first lot deeds for Manheim. The town was surveyed and drawn out by David Stoudt. A large, open square in the center of town was plotted as an important feature in the town (this was eventually named Market Square in 1872). Stiegel built a rather impressive two-and-half-story mansion at the northeast corner of Market Square on the corner of Prussian and High Streets. Prussian Street is now called Main Street but was originally named after Prussia, the German states that were then newly unified by King Frederick the Great. For many years, Manheim was called Stiegel Town by some.

In 1765, Stiegel moved his glass production to his new Manheim factory, which he called his "glasshouse." By 1770, the Stedmans had sold all of their town's land to Stiegel, whose successful glassmaking business helped build up the new town. Stiegel brought in talented foreign workers to produce and decorate his glassware. Stiegel's glasshouse produced both practical and beautifully decorated glassware, which was held in high esteem throughout the northeastern colonies. In addition to being shipped to Lancaster, Philadelphia, and several towns and cities across Pennsylvania, Stiegel's glass also went to New York, Boston, and Baltimore. The branding of a business was not as standardized back then as it is today, and Stiegel's glass business was advertised alternatively as the American Flint Glass Manufactory, Stiegel Glass Works, and the Glass Factory. Stiegel also ran successful gristmills in Manheim and at Elizabeth Furnace, from which he delivered many loads of flour to Philadelphia.

Henry Stiegel was a very devout Lutheran and was much concerned with church activities. In addition to attending services at the Warwick Lutheran Church in Brickerville, he provided a chapel in his homes at both Elizabeth Furnace and in Manheim for his workers. Being a fairly talented musician, Stiegel often led the church music and even services himself, but he would also bring in preachers from other congregations to conduct worship services at his chapels. His friend Pastor Henry Melchior Muhlenberg, later known as the father of the Lutheran church in the United States, visited Manheim on several occasions and preached to the small congregation in Stiegel's mansion. On September 18, 1769, Henry Melchior Muhlenberg helped to assemble the Manheim Lutheran Congregation in Stiegel's home. In either 1770 or 1771, Henry Muhlenberg's son Frederick Augustus Conrad Muhlenberg became pastor to the Manheim congregation as well as to those of White Oak, Brickerville, and Heidelberg (now Schaefferstown). It was during Frederick Muhlenberg's time in Manheim that the first church building was constructed. Frederick preached in Manheim until 1773, when he left for New York City and eventually became the first speaker of the US House of Representatives. Conflicting accounts exist as to Frederick Muhlenberg's influence on the first school in Manheim. In one account, he helped establish the first school; however, it is also recorded that before his pastoral duties began, a schoolmaster named Stephanus provided worship services and that the first schoolhouse was finished in 1767 and paid for by Stiegel's glass business. In either case, as was typical in colonial towns, the advent of school coincided with that of the church. It is unknown where Manheim's first school was located, but for some time it was operated out of a log house on North Charlotte Street and was known as the German School. In addition to his business, church, and school activities, Stiegel also helped organize the German Society of Pennsylvania in 1764, which helped immigrants under the redemptioner system, a harsh system of indentured servitude in which immigrants would pay back shipping companies for their Atlantic crossing with service upon arrival. Unfortunately, the exact terms of indenture were often negotiated after the immigrants arrived in the colonies, when the new arrivals had little leverage and no means of backing out of the deal.

Henry William Stiegel was a man of many interests and passions, most of which began with great success. Stiegel enjoyed his early victories without inhibition and loved to live in a manner above his means. By his own instigation, he was called the "Baron" and was known to have dressed and entertained like one. Sometime between 1768 and 1769, Stiegel built a tower on a hill called Thurmberg (German for "Tower Hill") in Schaefferstown, then known as Heidelberg. It was a rather unique pyramidal structure—50 feet square, 75 feet tall, and painted red. Furthering its peculiarity, a cannon mounted on the roof platform would discharge to provide a booming herald for the Baron and his guests as they would arrive and depart from the tower. This method of announcing his presence was also used at Elizabeth Furnace, with another cannon placed upon Cannon Hill. In Manheim, the Baron's orchestra would play on his rooftop at his coming as well.

Unfortunately, the combination of Stiegel's lavish lifestyle and the mounting financial depression of the colonies quickly gravitating toward revolution left him spiraling into financial ruin. Had Stiegel been able to sell off his numerous lots and estates located elsewhere, he could have remained in Manheim and continued to run his glassworks, which showed all signs of being able to continue to be a success despite the depressed economy. Unfortunately, that was not to be the case. Stiegel's copious debts became unmanageable. In 1773, Stiegel started a public lottery in an effort to accrue enough money to save him from his misfortune, but in the end, it amounted to just over £83—not enough to put a dent in his £10,000 debt. In the year between early 1774 and early 1775, Stiegel had lost all of his property in sheriff sales, and he had spent a few weeks in debtor's prison at the Philadelphia County Gaol (jail). His glass factory was bought by Michael Diffenderfer, who ran it for only a couple of years before shutting it down. All of Stiegel's remaining belongings were given over to his creditors, leaving him and his family with only their clothing and bedding not exceeding the value of 10 pounds. On Christmas Eve 1774, Stiegel was released from jail poor but free. His beloved glasshouse on the corner of Charlotte and Stiegel Streets was torn down in 1812 or 1813.

Stiegel and his family were allowed to move back to Elizabeth Furnace, although manufacturing was not in operation at the time, and Stiegel owned no rights to the property. During the Revolutionary War, it was leased to Robert Coleman, who fired up the furnaces to supply the colonial army with munitions. Stiegel worked for Coleman and joined a colonial militia. After the furnace was no longer needed for the war, Stiegel left Elizabeth Furnace to reside in the Brickerville church parsonage for about a year, then moved to the tower he had built in Heidelberg, then owned by his brother Anthony Stiegel. There, he became a schoolteacher. Around 1783, records of Baron Stiegel's whereabouts and activities greatly diminish, and what is left are only rumors regarding the end of his life. It is known that he ended up living with his nephew George Ege at Charming Forge in Womelsdorf and taught school there as well. Many believe he died in Charming Forge in 1785; however, this date is not without contention, as there are no records or grave to confirm it. Additionally, there are records from 1785 to 1788 of a Henry Stiegel being employed at the Mount Hope Furnace.

Stiegel's legacy in Manheim lives on both respectfully and infamously, and his grandfatherly presence is still felt throughout the town. Some say he haunts the building that was erected on the site of his mansion on Market Square, where at least one of the original walls still remains. Manheim Central High School honors Stiegel with the name used by the school's sports teams— the Barons. The Zion Lutheran Church, the land for which was given to the congregation by Stiegel for the price of five shillings and a yearly red rose, still gives a red rose to one of Stiegel's descendants each year. An impressive amount of information can be found about the details of Stiegel's friendships, financial records, advertisements, and personal dealings, but it is quite beyond the scope of this book to reproduce the whole of his life's story. We must give appropriate tribute to Henry William Stiegel, whose enterprising and ambitious spirit founded this great town. However, we must not mistake the Baron's story for the entirety of Manheim's. Much can be and has been said about Stiegel, his bold career, and his unfortunate downfall, but Manheim developed into its own entity, one that respects its intrepid founder while continuing to advance into its own separate history. As the community grew, other predominant early Americans resided in Manheim, many of whom will be introduced in the following chapters.

Manheim's lengthy history can be tangibly experienced through the numerous historical buildings throughout town. The span of Manheim's history is such that it has seen enough structures rise, fall, and be replaced by newer buildings that even the replacements are considered "old." However, some of the oldest brick buildings from the 1800s are still being in use today, while even earlier log cabins from the 1700s are said to lay dormant beneath modern siding. Two fully intact cabins from the area's earliest time are on display on High Street. The architectural styles in Manheim are diverse, with some of the predominant styles being Italianate, Pennsylvania German Vernacular, Gothic Revival, Eastlake, Second Empire, Renaissance Revival, Bungalow, and American Foursquare.

The intriguing story of Manheim continues long past the lifetime of the Baron, with historical buildings lining the town streets, rolling farmlands in the surrounding countryside (still occupied by "plain folk" families), and its small-town allure (although, incongruously, it is located beside the world's largest auto auction). Manheim grew and modernized and yet still carries its provincial charm, all of which is celebrated in the following pages. Welcome to Manheim! Or, as they say in German: *Willkommen!*

One

FOUNDATION TO THE MID-1800S

Following Henry Stiegel's departure from Manheim in 1775, Robert Morris and his family moved into Stiegel's mansion in 1777 and stayed there for a brief time. Morris was not only a signer of the Declaration of Independence but also a principle financier of the American Revolution. While Morris was in the mansion, John Hancock, Gen. Horatio Gates, and other members of Congress visited him in Manheim at various times during the Revolutionary War. Across the street lived Richard Bache, a colonial postmaster and the successor of his father-in-law Benjamin Franklin. Surgeon General of the US Army Dr. Joseph Shippen also lived in Manheim at this time.

In 1805, Maj. Gen. Samuel Peter Heintzelman was born in Manheim. He spent most of his life as a professional soldier, traveling across the United States and documenting his travels in his diaries. In 1857, he participated in the foundation of the Sonora Exploring and Mining Company in Arizona, a venture that led him to document life in the Southwest during that time.

As the area's population began to increase, so did literacy and education. The free public school system came to Manheim in 1833. The original German schoolhouse became the Central School. In 1836, the Upper School was built on the north side of Lebanon Road, and the Lower School was constructed on West Ferdinand Street. Manheim's first newspaper was said to have been started by Jacob Stauffer, who began printing in Manheim in 1830; however, his business was short-lived in Manheim, and he soon moved to Mount Joy. John M. Ensminger is said to be the "Father of Manheim Journalism." He created the first single-sheet newspaper in 1841; it was called *The Sun*. Records are conflicting about the exact dates of its evolution, but the paper changed names to the *Weekly Planet and Rapho Banner*, then the *Manheim Planet and Banner*, and finally the *Manheim Sentinel*.

Manheim was incorporated as a borough on April 16, 1838, with a population of 365 residents.

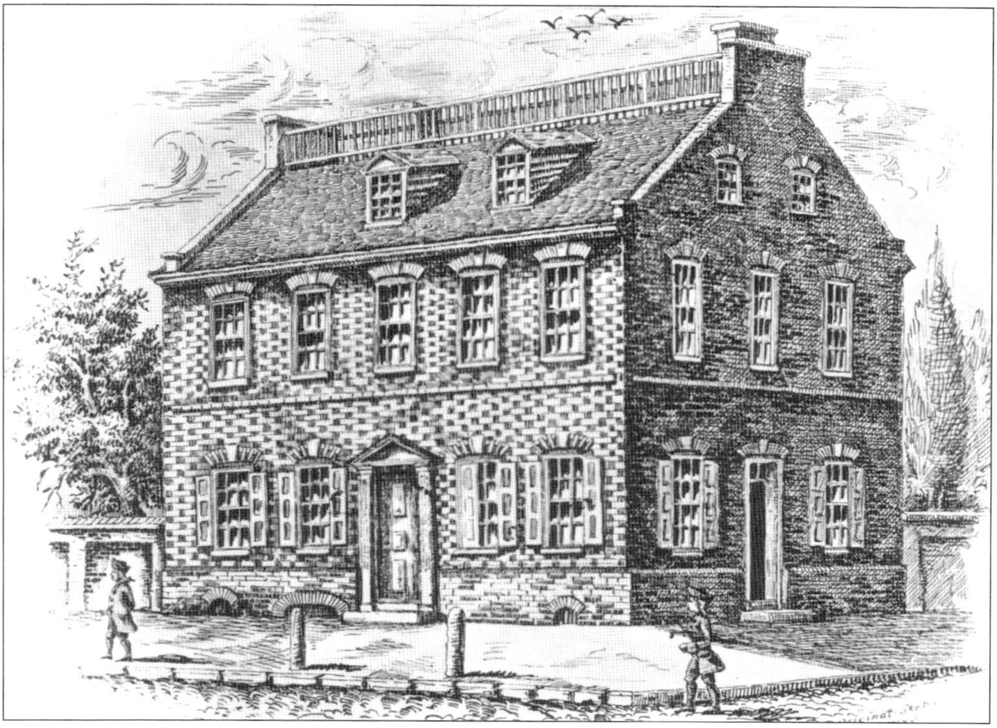

This was Henry Stiegel's mansion, which he built between 1763 and 1764 on the northwest corner of Market Square at the intersection of Prussian (now Main) and High Streets. It was two and a half stories and built in the Georgian style. The structure was partially torn down and rebuilt between 1865 and 1875, when John Arndt made the first major changes to it. His son Henry Arndt later made further changes. According to the Lancaster County Historic Resources Inventory (LCHRI), the north gable and some parts of the rear wall of the original mansion remain. Although this is not noted in the database, the south exterior wall, which has a historical dedication plaque, still has some of the original brickwork. The LCHRI database notes that the interior of the mansion was known to be "unusual" but does not explain in what way; however, Stiegel could be quite flamboyant and extravagant in his lifestyle. Stiegel's mansion was lavish for the time and included a widow's walk on the roof, where his band would perform concerts and announce his arrival and departure. (Both, MHS.)

Sometime after John Arndt remodeled Henry Stiegel's mansion almost to the point of not being recognizable, his son Henry Arndt further contributed to the transformation when he removed and dispersed the original tiles to his friends and family. These tiles, installed by Stiegel, were decorated with biblical scenes and can now be found in various collections. (MHS.)

Today, the southeast wall of the existing building facing High Street contains brickwork that is a remnant of the original mansion. On this wall is a historic plaque that was placed there by the Order of Baron Von Stiegel, a social club founded in 1927, to document some of the building's history. (MHS.)

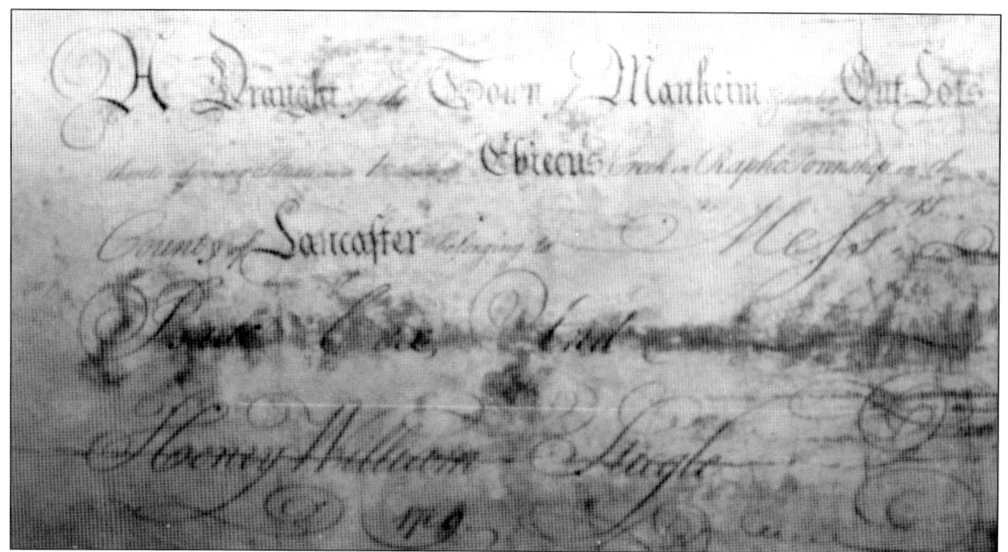

This is a detail of the original Manheim map and indenture document of the Stedmans and Henry William Stiegel. Curiously, in this document Chiques Creek, which borders the town of Manheim on the east and south, is called Ebiecus Creek. Also note the alternative spelling of Stiegel as "Stiegle." (MHS.)

Henry Stiegel's office/storeroom was located on the northwest section of the square on the corner of North Charlotte and West High Streets and faced his mansion across the square on the corner of East High and North Prussian Streets. This building was torn down in 1910. Interestingly, several of Stiegel's ledgers—that he no doubt wrote in this office—have been preserved. (MHS.)

There is no exact image of the glasshouse built by Henry Stiegel in 1763. However, this drawing was done by Bill McComsey based on historical records and other known glass factories. According to some records, the cupola was over 100 feet high, and a six-horse carriage could enter and turn around inside the building. Located on the corner of West Stiegel and South Charlotte Streets, the building was torn down around 1813. (MHS.)

Stiegel-type glass was originally an imitation of glass products being imported from Europe at the time. All of the Stiegel glass was blown and then decorated by three styles: pattern-molded, cut and engraved, and enameled. The Daisy Diamond, daisy in square, and hexagon pattern molds are considered to be unique to Stiegel's glassworks. The first advertisement for his Manheim glassworks was printed in the *Pennsylvania Gazette* in 1765. (MHS.)

Henry W. Stiegel's glasswork became varied and artistic. In addition to engraving, he also enameled some of his glass in bright colors such as blue, green, amber, and amethyst. After Stiegel's business was up and running, he eventually called it the American Flint Glass Manufactory and built a second glasshouse in Manheim. (MHS.)

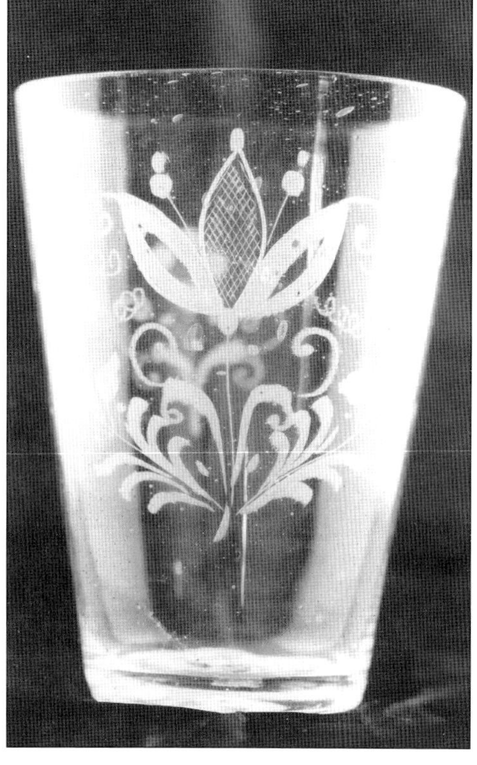

This flint glass cup was created in Stiegel's second Manheim glasshouse. It is an example of Stiegel's shallow-cut copper-wheel engraving. Stiegel's engravings contained traditional Pennsylvania Dutch folk art styles, which can still be seen in the area today. Some of these familiar motifs include (but are not limited to) tulips, hearts, birds, vines, and wreaths. (Not all Stiegel-type glass was made by Stiegel, but the name represents that particular style.) (MHS.)

Chiques (pronounced "Chickies" and is often spelled as such) Creek is a fairly robust creek running along the east and south side of the borough. Today, one may still hear those with a Pennsylvania Dutch accent call a creek a "crick." Two of the earliest area records call it Checasolunga (a variation of Chiquesalunga) and Sheckasalungo in 1724. A colonial minute book from 1733 states that the Native Americans living in the area were called the Shecassalunga. Various other spellings for both the creek and the tribe can be found throughout the years. To further confuse the issue, it was also known as Ebiecus (or Ebyes/Eby's) Creek on Henry Stiegel's early town maps. It is not known why Stiegel would have named it as such on his maps, as it was already well established as being the Chiquesalunga. Because of the number of artifacts found in the area, it is believed that the land was home to Native Americans; however, most of them seemed to have left before the European colonists arrived.

The Fasig House is a fabulous artifact of early Manheim and a historical treasure for the community. Although the exact date of this log cabin's construction is not known, it was built in the 1700s and originally located at 32 South Charlotte Street. After being gifted to the Manheim Historical Society, it was dismantled and reconstructed on High Street, where it currently resides and is home to numerous artifacts from the 1700s and 1800s. The house is named after the several generations of the Fasig family who lived there, including the last resident of the house, Anna Fasig. It was used as a religious meeting place, and the congregations of the Trinity Evangelical Congregational Church and the United Brethren Church in Christ sprung from those early meetings. There are other 18th- and 19th-century log homes still in Manheim, although most of them have been clad in modern siding and undergone other alterations. (Both, MHS.)

The Keath House is a wonderful example of an early Colonial-era German log cabin. The Keath House currently sits next to the Fasig House on High Street and was also moved from its original location. Unlike the Fasig House, it was moved whole in the 1990s. Records exist for the original property going back to 1773, when Henry Stiegel sold the property to Henry Hantz and his heirs. (Photograph by the author.)

The 1983 remodeling of this house at 24 Market Square shows the original log construction that lay hidden beneath the siding. It is believed that many houses throughout Manheim still have their original log frames underneath modern siding. (MHS.)

This home is known as the Barthold-Guion House and is located at 122 North Charlotte Street. The oak and chestnut house beneath the modern siding is believed to be original; it dates to before the Revolutionary War. While the original structure's history still needs to be verified, there are official records showing that the property was seized from Henry Stiegel and sold by John Ferree, sheriff of Lancaster County, in 1775. (MHS.)

The German Lutheran congregation was brought to Manheim by Rev. Henry Melchior Muhlenberg when he visited Henry Stiegel and preached in the chapel in Stiegel's mansion in 1769. Frederick Augustus Conrad Muhlenberg (shown here), son of Henry Melchior Muhlenberg, became pastor of Manheim's Lutheran congregation in either 1770 or 1771. In addition to working in Manheim, he was pastor of the White Oak, Brickerville, and Heidelberg congregations. In 1779, he was nominated to the Continental Congress. As president of the Pennsylvania Convention, he helped to ratify the new federal constitution and later became the first Speaker of the House of Representatives. (MHS.)

Henry "Baron" Stiegel gave Lot 220 to the local community of Lutherans for the price of five shillings and a red rose (to be given every June). Although the yearly gift of a rose may seem unusually sentimental today, it was not a totally uncommon arrangement in those days in England and the New World. This lot had been intended to be a "free" church lot since the original mapping of Manheim. It is unknown how many times, if at all, the payment of the rose was given to Stiegel and his family; however, in 1892, J.H. Sieling proposed that the tradition be reinstated and a festival held every year, with the first recipient being John C. Stiegel. To this day, the congregation still gives one of Stiegel's descendants a red rose every year during the Festival of the Red Rose. The wooden Zion Lutheran Church was built on the corner of Wolf and High Streets on Lot 220 in 1770 (or possibly 1772). (MHS.)

These very old tombstones in the Zion Lutheran Church cemetery display beautiful examples of common Pennsylvania Dutch tombstone motifs. On the tombstone at left, the hourglass at the top represents the passing of time and was a common engraving before 1800. Flowers are the most common symbol among Pennsylvania Dutch tombstones and, in general, feature heavily in artwork. However, the snake on a column on Johan Andreas Bartruf's stone (in the image at left) is an uncommon symbol. Bartruf was an innkeeper on Prussian (Main) Street. (Both, MHS.)

This beautifully illuminated Bible was presented to Rev. Raymond Foellner at the Zion Evangelical Lutheran Church in Manheim. The Pennsylvania Dutch style of the script and the manuscript illustrations is called Fraktur. This style has been around since at least the 1760s and continues to be a recognizable style of Pennsylvania Dutch culture today. (MHS.)

On the northwest corner of Market Square, beside Prussian Street, were the Manheim Dental Parlors. This brick building was constructed in the Georgian style and was the home of Richard Bache between 1777 and 1778. Bache was the son-in-law of Benjamin Franklin and became postmaster general. This building was later replaced by the Manheim National Bank. (MHS.)

The home of Emmanuel Deyer (1760–1836) stood at 128 South Main Street. It is believed that about 65 percent of the original facade still exists, with the rest of the building constructed around 1840. Deyer was a carpenter and cabinetmaker and one of the original directors of the Manheim Fire Company in 1812. He is buried under the St. Paul's United Church of Christ parking lot (see page 27). (Photograph by the author.)

The Black Horse Inn at 25 South Prussian (Main) Street was built by John Heintzelman, son of Hieronymus (Jerome) Heintzelman, in 1817. Records indicate that John Heintzelman bought this property in 1796. He was also a clockmaker. This current Italianate-style building was constructed around 1905 after the first structure was razed by Simeon Guilford Summy in 1891 (see page 51). (Photograph by the author.)

Records are conflicting about when this house was built and which Heintzelman bought the property shown below; however, it is known that by 1805, Peter and Ann Heintzelman lived there, and it is where their son Samuel Peter Heintzelman was born. Peter Heintzelman's father, Hieronymus (Jerome) Heintzelman, was a German immigrant and original Manheim settler who bought land directly from Henry William Stiegel. Samuel Heintzelman began his military career when he was recommended by James Buchanan to the Military Academy at West Point. His military career took him all over the country, including to stations in Kansas, Florida, New York, and California, and he went up the ranks to become major general. He participated in both the Mexican War and the Civil War. He also was a part of an expedition around Cape Horn to California. Portions of this house still remain at 24 (and possibly 22) South Main Street, but it has undergone a number of additions and alterations. (Right, MHS; below, photograph by the author.)

25

This coverlet is a fantastic artifact from the 1800s. In the early to mid-19th century, Henry Brosey, John Brosey, and Adam Danner were Manheim weavers who provided woven cloth, blankets, and carpets to the town. They got their dyed wool from Martin Rudisil. A younger coverlet from the late 1800s is also owned by the MHS and is on display in the Fasig House. (Photograph by the author.)

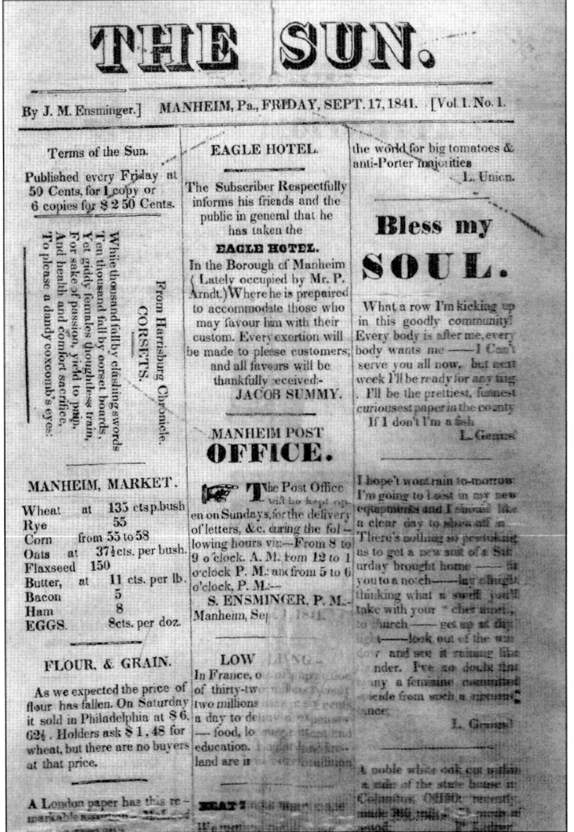

John M. Ensminger, the "Father of Manheim Journalism," started Manheim's second print shop in 1841 (or possibly 1838) and created a publication called *The Sun*. Later, he would develop *The Sun* into Manheim's first full newspaper, the *Weekly Planet and Rapho Banner*. A curious little blurb with the headline "Bless My Soul" is in the right column in this image. It is attributed to "L. Genius" and is about causing quite a stir in the community and how the writer (in first person) will be "ready for anything" next week. (MHS.)

The first church on this site was dedicated in 1769 by a congregation in the German Reformed Church. This building, currently still in use as St. Paul's United Church of Christ, was constructed in 1852. The church was built in the Gothic Revival style and features Gothic arched stained-glass windows and a gold-leafed orb and arrow weather vane at the top of the steeple. At some point in modern times, the graveyard was paved over to create a parking lot, and the tombstones are being stored in the basement. (MHS.)

This photograph shows Abraham Hostetter's water-powered mill that was built in 1829 on South Oak Street. Behind the building was the Manheim Electric Company, which first brought electricity to Manheim in 1896. After having several owners over the years, the mill eventually came to be owned by B.R. Hollinger in 1906 and was the site of his lumber and feed business, which then changed names to Raymond W. Hollinger and Sons after his death. Before all this, though, it was near the site of an earlier mill owned and operated by Peter Longenecker between 1773 and 1780. (MHS.)

One of Manheim's historical treasures is Shearer's covered bridge, which crosses Chiques Creek and is currently located on Adele Avenue by the high school, farm show complex, and Manheim Veterans Memorial Park. It was originally constructed in 1847 by Jacob Clare but had to be rebuilt in 1855. It was built about four miles away and moved to its current location in 1971. This wooden double Burr arch truss bridge is unique in that it is the only covered bridge in Lancaster County that is entirely red and one of only three that have horizontal side boards and windows. (Both, photograph by the author.)

Two

MID-1800S TO THE MID-1900S

This period of Manheim's history brought many changes to the town as the community developed, businesses sprouted up, and the people boldly faced the Civil War and two World Wars. Since its inception, Manheim has been a manufacturing town. It became a trade center for the agricultural land surrounding it, and the town itself has been home to numerous manufacturers over the centuries. From the original Stiegel glassworks to the cigars that dominated manufacturing after the Civil War to the industrial supplies and machine parts still produced in town today, Manheim has long prided itself on industry. Additional areas of manufacturing also included clockmaking, making garments, blacksmithing, and much more.

In the 1860s, the railroad lines that came to town fueled transportation in and out of Manheim for both passengers and cargo. A variety of 19th-century entertainments could be found throughout Manheim, which was renowned for its musicians. Manheim residents were often serenaded by wandering quartettes and ocarina groups during the evening. Occasionally, traveling theater troupes would play in town. The Arndt building, which was built over the remnants of Stiegel's mansion, hosted suppers, dances, and plays. Manheim founded its own school district and separated from Rapho Township's district in 1855. In late 1800s, telephones and electricity were introduced to Manheim.

Manheim, like so many other towns across America, did not go unscathed in wartime. During the Civil War, 179 men from Manheim and the surrounding areas joined the Union army. At one point, Manheim became a refuge for residents who fled the nearby town of Columbia in fear of the advancing Confederate army. After World War I, Prussian Street was renamed Main Street for patriotic reasons revolving around the United States' conflict with Germany. During World War II, Manheim participated in scrap-metal collection efforts as 988 Manheim men and women went off in service of the US military.

Manheim celebrated its success and long history with a weeklong festival called Old Home Week from June 30 through July 4, 1912. This celebration was a community-wide project filled with pomp, decoration, and festivities. Historical sites were marked and dated, and hundreds of flags, electric string lights, and Japanese lanterns were hung across town. In Market Square, 22 large pillars were erected to decorate the vendor space. Parades, concerts, and speeches were also held.

In 1857, the original wooden Zion Lutheran Church was torn down and replaced with this new brick building. The congregation outgrew this new church only 34 years later. In order to construct a larger structure and not disturb the graves in the cemetery, the third (and current) church was built on the opposite corner of the lot on the corner of Hazel Street. Many of the bricks from this church were reused to construct the new one (see page 57). (MHS.)

In 1872, the square in Manheim was officially named Market Square. Around 1912, porches began to be built on the front of the houses around the square. While many of these buildings are still standing and still carry historical charm, they have had a number of alterations, rendering this view of Market Square recognizable yet different than the one of today. (MHS.)

Between 1865 and 1875, Henry Arndt constructed a new building over Stiegel's mansion, and it was built in the Victorian Italianate style. In the 1950s or 1960s, a new first-floor storefront was added. Today, the southeast wall facing High Street contains original brickwork from the mansion. The building has been home to numerous businesses over the years, including the Phoenix Twirling Corp., a baton twirling group directed by John Bunteman Jr. It has been suggested that the building may be haunted, possibly by the Baron himself. (Photograph by the author.)

In 1893, Stiegel Castle, No. 166, R.C.E. installed a memorial fountain for Henry William Stiegel in the Zion Lutheran Church's cemetery. The fountain base has the words "FIDELITY, VALOR, HONOR" inscribed on it. During the time of this book's writing in 2020, the cemetery was going through renovations and conservation. (MHS.)

A.R. Reiff was one of many cigar manufacturers in town in the late 1800s. In 1871, he also had a grocery store. Reiff was also known as being an excellent snare drummer and was one of the charter members of Manheim Lodge 587. (MHS.)

A United Brethren Church on the left and the Prussian House on the right frame this view looking down North Prussian Street. Records indicate that in 1873, gutters were added to the streets of town; therefore, based on the gutter present on the left side of the image, this photograph was most likely taken after that date. (MHS.)

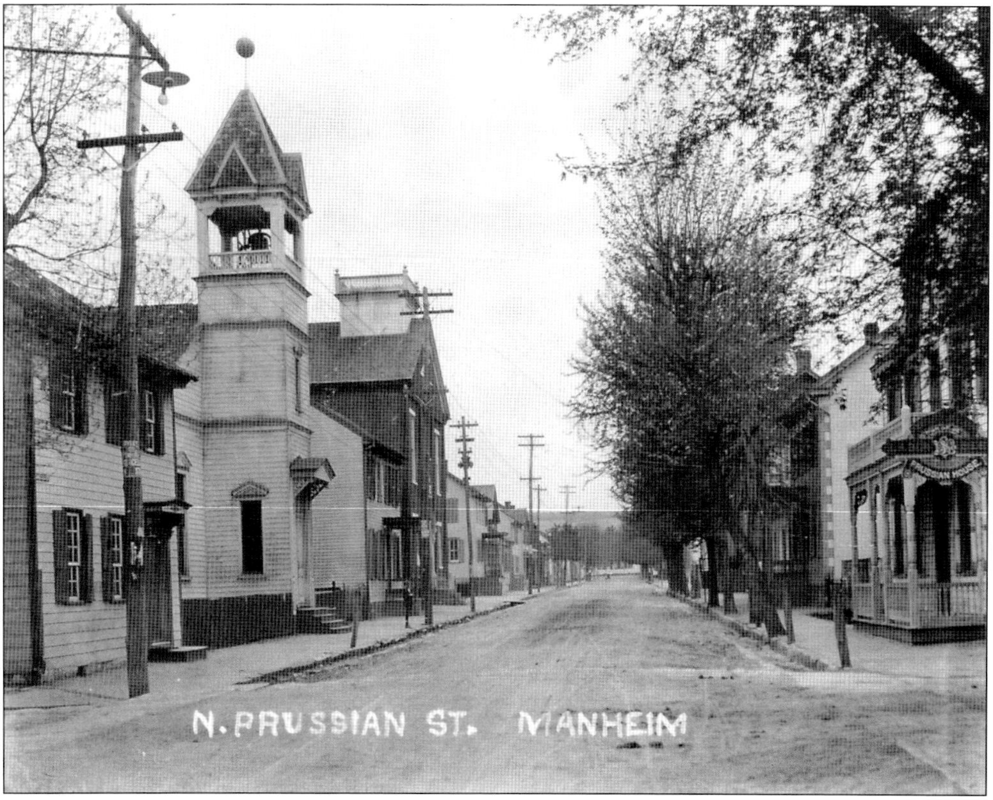

This clock, owned by the MHS, was made by George
Eby, son of Jacob Eby. George was a clockmaker and
merchant in Manheim in the mid-1800s on Prussian
Street (now Main Street). He was also one of the first
councilmen when Manheim was incorporated as a
borough in 1838. The clock is still in working order today
and sits among the artifacts on display at the Harry B.
Shearer Heritage Center. (Photograph by the author.)

The first railroad tracks were laid down in Manheim
in the 1860s, and this station was completed in 1881.
It is believed by some to have been designed by the
famous Victorian architect Frank Furness. He was also
the architect of many Reading Railroad stations. The
station serviced goods and passengers traveling to and
from Lancaster, Lebanon, Columbia, Reading, and Jersey
City. The station is still standing and is owned by the
MHS. It serves as a home for a small model railroad and
museum and is used for community events. (MHS.)

The Manheim railroad station faced its share of drama over the years. In the spring of 1896, there was a massive train wreck at the station. "The Night Buck" hit a boxcar, causing the engine to fall over. In 1905, severe flooding tore up some of the track, which needed to be fixed. More misfortune flared up at the station when there was a train holdup in 1962. (MHS.)

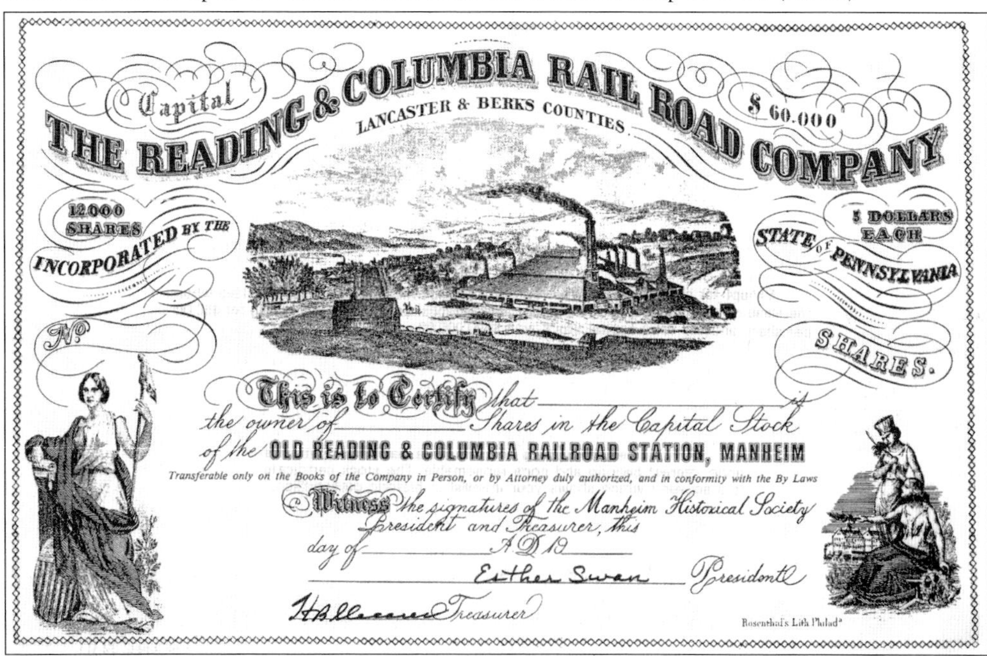

This souvenir stock certificate closely resembles a real stock certificate of the Reading & Columbia Rail Road from 1862, when the company was established. At that time, there were 12,000 shares available for $50 each. (MHS.)

The American House hotel was built in 1869 by J.S. Henry on the corner of South Charlotte Street and Railroad Avenue, near the train station. In addition to guest rooms, the hotel featured a barroom, dining room, and parlors and had its own water spring in the basement. By 1912, it was owned by William C. Lefevre and outfitted with electricity, heat, and telephones. (MHS.)

This c. 1875 drawing shows E.B. Bomberger's mill, which was located on the east end of town near Chiques Creek at Mill and Oak Streets. Bomberger bought this mill in 1866 from Abraham Hostetter, who built it in 1829 (see pages 28 and 29). Bomberger was also one of the incorporators of Fairview Cemetery. (MHS.)

This photograph shows the Baumgardner family outside of their bakery at 40 North Charlotte Street. From left to right are Mae Baumgardner, Chas. Rickert, Paul Baumgardner, John Baumgardner, John's youngest brother (unidentified), a Mrs. Baumgardner, and Jere Baumgardner (standing near the horse). This building no longer exists, and Coleman Alley now runs alongside the property. (MHS.)

On the far left of this snowy view of the square is a house believed to have been a very old log cabin that was remodeled in the late 1800s. It is still standing today. To its right is Baron Stiegel's old office and storeroom. To the right of that is Trinity Evangelical Congregational Church and the Danner Building (in the center of the square). (MHS.)

The three-story Danner Building stands in the center of the north side of the square. This brick building was constructed in 1882 to replace the two-story clapboard structure that was George H. Danner's original store established in 1862. The arched windows, brick corbeling on the exterior, and a corbeled roof overhang are still recognizable today, but the large triangular pediment has been removed. (MHS.)

George Danner (1834–1917) was an avid collector of artifacts and antiques who eventually opened up the third floor of his building as a museum once a week. Danner stated in his will that the store and museum should remain open after his death. Unfortunately, his final wishes were unable to be fulfilled despite years of effort by the trustees. In 1935, Milton Hershey bought Danner's collection of artifacts, which can still be viewed in the Hershey Story Museum. In 1941, the store permanently closed. (MHS.)

This log house was located on the corner of South Charlotte and West Ferdinand Streets. At left is Aaron Danner (1837–1925), who published poetry in the *Manheim Sentinel* under the name Sinceritas, among other accomplishments. He was also a councilman. At right is George Danner. Daniel Danner (1803–1881), father of Aaron and George, had his wood-turning shop here. (MHS.)

Samuel Ensminger started his apothecary business in 1798 on the southeast corner of the square. When compared to an older sketch of this home, this photograph appears to show that the house was remodeled from an older version. Harry C. Stauffer and his wife were the last residents who lived here before the house was torn down in 1925 to make way for the construction of the Keystone National Bank. (MHS.)

This view of the town square looking toward the southwest is believed to have been taken in the mid-19th century (before 1880). A carriage is parked on the dirt road and surrounded by several buildings that are no longer in existence. Just to the right of the carriage, in the distance, are Stiegel's office and storeroom. (MHS.)

Isaac Miller and his wife relax outside of their home at 231 South Cherry Street, with the Miller Cigar Factory on the right. This photograph was taken around 1890. The Millers' daughter Jennie sold candy and hosiery from this house until well into her later years. Note the dirt streets and wood-plank sidewalks. (MHS.)

The original Manheim public school building (above) was constructed on the corner of East High Street and what was to become North Hazel Street. It received a major addition in 1868 on the left side, which is shown below. After this renovation, a new bell that weighed 200 pounds was installed in the steeple. During this time, the road along the right side of the school did not yet appear to exist; when the road was constructed, it was originally named Hay Alley and later called Hazel Street. The current building replaced this one in 1914, but the house at far left in the below photograph is still standing today. (Both, MHS.)

It is believed that this photograph is of Calvin Sahm, who grew up to be a notable singer in Ohio. Behind him is a grocery store on the corner of West Ferdinand and South Charlotte Streets. At various times, this store was owned by Herbert George, George Seabold, A.D. Sahm (Calvin's father), and Charles Albright. (MHS.)

The B.S. Colten Horse Shoer and Blacksmith shop was located on the corner of East Stiegel and Wolf Streets across from John W. Koch's Wheelwright Shop. This building housed M.M. Bowser's blacksmith shop from 1892 to 1910. Eventually, the building burned down in a fire. (MHS.)

This large brick and stucco house at 2 West Stiegel Street sits on the corner of South Main Street. It was built in 1880 in the Second Empire style and features a mansard roof with corbels under the cornice. (Photograph by the author.)

This impressive home at 3 West Stiegel Street, on the corner of South Main Street, has an eclectic style that is described as both Queen Anne/Colonial Revival and Châteauesque. According to a newspaper announcement, this house was built in 1902 by florist E.P. Hostetter. However, there are other records that indicate it was built around 1890 by Ezra Reist. In 1912, there was a porch on the Stiegel Street side that wrapped around to Main Street. (Photograph by the author.)

The 73 South Main Street address has been home to drugstores in Manheim for nearly 150 years. The first was opened in 1878 by Dr. H.A. Mulliner, and it was later owned by Josiah Landis, who sold it to H.F. Ruhl Sr. Ruhl opened his drugstore, shown in these pictures, in 1891. H.F. Ruhl Jr. took over the store from his father in 1946 and ran it for many years. The original building is no longer there, but in its place is Sloan's Pharmacy, which has been serving the Manheim community since 1983. The Sloan's sign on Main Street displays a mortar and pestle very similar to the one in front of Ruhl's in the above photograph. In the below photograph, the man is believed to be H.F. Ruhl Sr., although this is unverified. (Both, Thomas A. Young.)

In the late 1800s, Litzenberger Hardware, owned by Willoughby Litzenberger, was located in the center of Market Square. Litzenberger and Alfred Deyer ran the business in 1874 as the Litzenberger and Deyer Store, but Deyer retired in 1879. The exterior photograph above was taken between the late 1800s and early 1900s while the interior photograph below was taken later, as indicated by the date—September 4, 1920—in the advertisement at left. The store later became Longenecker's Hardware, and after that, it was the location of A & M Pizza, a much-loved restaurant. In 1998, the structure burned down but was rebuilt by A & M Pizza. (Both, MHS.)

On July 18, 1894, the Dunlaps hosted a large picnic in their yard. A gaggle of children participated in a potato race. Potato races were popular events from the mid-19th century until about the 1930s in Great Britain, the United States, and Australia. (MHS.)

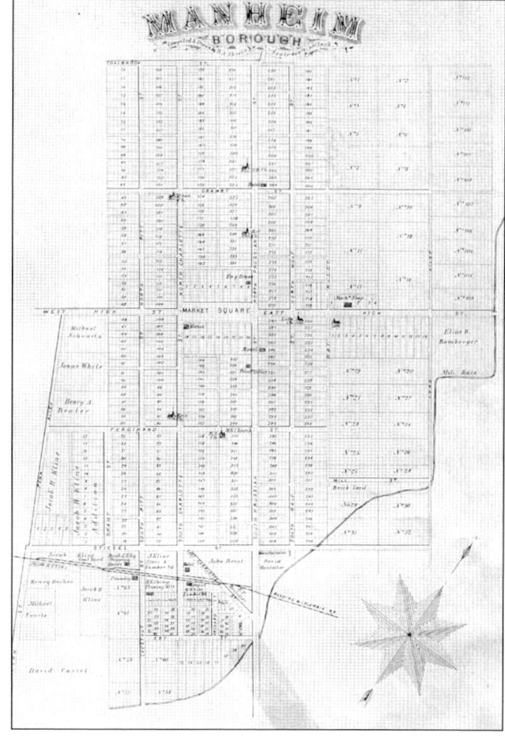

This map shows the borough of Manheim as it appeared in 1875. Several locations mentioned in this chapter can be found on this map. It is interesting to note that at this time, today's Hazel Street was called Hay Alley, and it appears that the current Linden Street was Long Alley. East Charlotte Street is now called New Charlotte Street, and Prussian Street is now Main Street. (MHS.)

Manheim's first Trinity Evangelical Congregational Church was located on the corner of North Charlotte and West Gramby Streets around 1835. The congregation originally stemmed from religious meetings held at the Fasig House (see page 18). This Trinity Evangelical Congregational Church, located on the northwest corner of Market Square, was built in 1883 in the Romanesque Revival style. (MHS.)

The first Episcopal denomination services on record in Manheim occurred in 1849 at the Mount Hope Estate. After the denomination grew in popularity, St. Paul's Episcopal Church was built in 1869 on South Charlotte Street. This church is of unusual construction—it is in the First Gothic Revival style but made out of wood. (MHS.)

Abraham Kauffman was a predominant figure in Manheim. He was elected to the House of Representatives in 1836, 1837, and 1843. He also helped to establish the Manheim National Bank. In 1869, Kauffman gifted three acres of land just outside of the borough line to the borough of Manheim with the direction that it be used for a public park for the community. Although Route 72 (Main Street) currently runs beside the park, at the time, the old route that was here was closed by John Gibble, who owned the land on which the road was located. In 1870, a borough committee established a means for transportation to and from the park. Kauffman Park was a great destination for community members for a few decades, but eventually, it became unused and overgrown. In 1945, the Rotary Club completed some hefty maintenance in the park. Route 72 was constructed in 1953; it spilt the park in two, with a walkway under the road connecting the two parts. Presently, the main portion of the park contains a restaurant, a miniature golf course, and a spring that flows into a small creek. (Both, MHS.)

The spring pictured here is called Indian Springs and is located within Kauffman Park. In the 1770s, Native Americans would use this location for gatherings and other activities. The history plaque at the site says that in 1915, the spring was "walled in with the sponsorship of H.H. Bertheizel and the employees of Eisenlohr Cigar Factory." Later, a bandstand and pavilion were added. In 1989, the borough leased the park to Kenny Shank, who established a restaurant and golf course on the property. The restaurant and golf course now have new owners who call the establishment The Shack. Currently, the spring and its Greek temple–style pavilion are part of the 12th hole on the golf course. (Both, MHS.)

In 1876, Simeon Guilford Summy, a Swiss immigrant, bought the Black Horse Inn on Prussian Street (see page 24). His successful enterprise outgrew the location, and in 1881, he built a hotel and restaurant next door (shown here) and called it the Summy House. Summy helped to locate Manheim's stockyards and became a member of the American Mechanics. The Summy House served Manheim for over 100 years. It is currently split up into multiple rental spaces. (MHS.)

This photograph is of Elizabeth Will Young (1859–1956) dressed in a Christmas-season costume. This costume may have been a part of Manheim's celebration of the very old German tradition of "Belsnickel." The Belsnickel was a character that was a cross between St. Nicholas and Krampus. A newspaper article from 1910 announced the celebration of Belsnickel with masqueraders in costumes that the paper described as "grotesque and some very funny." (MHS.)

The Washington House tavern was built on the corner of South Charlotte and High Streets on Market Square. According to the Pennsylvania Historic Resource Survey, a tavern may have existed in this location before 1800. In 1817, it was owned by Jacob Meyer. In 1877, Martin Schreider was the owner. In 1895, a party was held here by the manager at the time, Bailey, to celebrate electric lighting in Manheim, which had just been turned on for the first time. Chief Burgess Bomberger, the town council, and the Germania Band attended. Apparently on slow days, in addition to human residents and visitors, well-behaved dogs were also welcome at the tavern. (Both, MHS.)

This large Second Empire brick home with a mansard roof stands at 101 South Charlotte Street on the corner of West Ferdinand Street. It was built in approximately 1880 and was owned by the Fisher family. Later, it became the Frey (also spelled Fry) residence and was a boardinghouse called Mizpah in the early 1900s. (MHS.)

Frederick Loercher, an immigrant from Wurttemberg, Germany, started a brewery here in 1871 and operated it until his death in 1886. The house was built in the Pennsylvania German Vernacular style. It is still recognizable on the corner of the East Gramby and North Wolf Streets, although the rest of the street looks quite different—and much more developed—today. (MHS.)

Abram Kline (also alternatively recorded as Abraham Kline) was an influential entrepreneur in the late 1800s in Manheim. He owned a large lumber and hardware store near the railroad tracks, as shown here. Kline lived on one corner of Market Square. He was burgess of Manheim in 1873. Kline's business was one of the first companies to install telephones when they arrived in town in 1889. (MHS.)

This view of the square facing northeast offers a glimpse into what the square would have looked like in the 1800s. The building at far left is where Henry Stiegel's mansion was once located. It was mostly demolished and rebuilt into the structure shown here, often called the Arndt Building, which is still standing today. The building to its right was the impressive three-story residence of Abram Kline. It was razed in 1910 and replaced by the Faith Independent Church and, later, the Salem United Brethren Church (see page 77). (MHS.)

Keystone National Bank was established in 1887. Around 1894, it was located in this building on the southeast side of the square, as shown in this 1912 photograph. This location is a couple of doors up from the bank building that would replace it in 1925. This bank and the building on the right (the Graybill residence) were later taken down to provide space for the bank's drive-through. (MHS.)

Around 1890, Peter Arnold bought the property at 122 East High Street; he most likely built the house shown here, which he used for his coachworks business. In 1907, Elam "Zimmy" Zimmerman bought a Reo automobile and fell in love with cars. He opened Manheim's first garage in this building. (Photograph by the author.)

Decoration Day, now known as Memorial Day, was officially established in 1868 as a day of remembrance and celebration. In this 1894 photograph, children and adults alike celebrate the country's fallen heroes in a march across town. (MHS.)

This 1895 Decoration Day parade is marching through Market Square. The Arndt Building in the center and the Abram Kline residence on the right frame East High Street, where the road heads northeast and turns into Doe Run Road as it crosses Chiques Creek on the edge of the borough. (MHS.)

The third and current Zion Evangelical Lutheran Church was constructed in 1891 on the property that Henry Stiegel gave to the church, but this new building was placed on the corner of Hazel Street instead of the original spot on the corner of Wolf Street. The church, built in the Gothic style, features a high tower, sandstone lintels, a corbelled brick cornice, and Gothic arch stained-glass windows on the first floor with round stained-glass windows above. The year after this new church was built, the congregation reinstated the annual giving of a red rose to one of Stiegel's descendants, as was directed in the original deed from 1772. Dr. J.H. Sieling, who proposed the continuation of giving a red rose to Stiegel's descendants, is standing by the entrance in the above photograph that shows the construction of the church. The construction workers were employees of Lewis Barthold. The architect is not known. (Both, MHS.)

This turn-of-the-20th-century photograph is of a Zion Lutheran Church choir picnic. In the carriage on the right, the driver is Harry Stormfeltz, with Prof. Urban Hershey next to him. (MHS.)

This photograph was taken in front of the old Manheim Post Office at the end of the Spanish-American War in 1898. The model ship in the center is of the battleship *Maine*, which was sunk during the war. A big parade was put on in Manheim as part of the memorial celebration. (MHS.)

58

In this view looking southeast along South Charlotte Street at the intersection of West Ferdinand Street, the Frey residence is at left, and a home that was used as a grocery store by multiple owners over the years is on the right (see page 43). This photograph was taken around 1900. (MHS.)

On the west side of South Charlotte Street was Hope Episcopal Church, which later became St. Paul's Episcopal Church. Beyond the church on the left is Cal Yetter's log cabin, which no longer exists. (MHS.)

This scene at the railroad station was a common sight around 1900. The railroad station became not only a hub for transportation but a place for the community to visit, people-watch, and see the trains coming and going. The hustle and bustle of the station was a fun attraction for local residents. (MHS.)

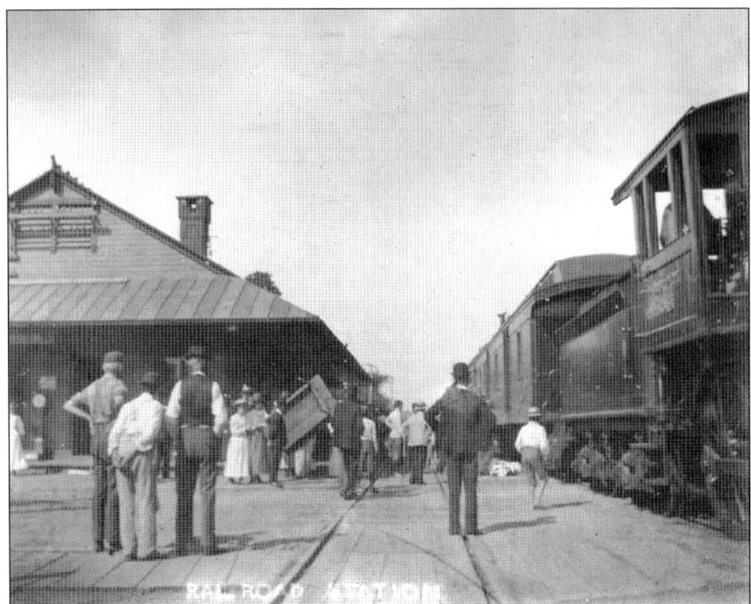

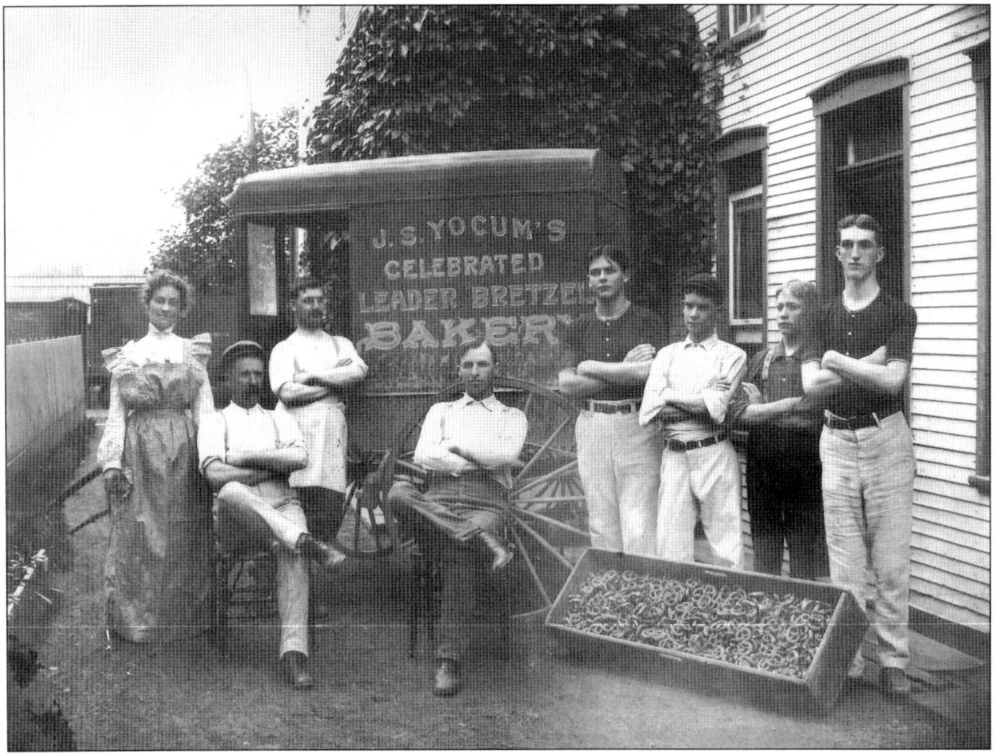

Bretzel is the German word for "pretzel." The Leader Bretzels advertised on J.S. Yocum's carriage are being proudly displayed in a wooden box in this photograph that also features, from left to right, Jerome S. Yocum's wife, Jerome S. Yocum (seated), Ezra Zartman, William Heisey (seated), Jerome Long, Charles Leedom, Israel Witmyer, and Charles Fass. Jerome Yocum opened his bakery on Grant Street in 1884. He became the proprietor of the American House for a short time but then went back to the bakery business. (MHS.)

This photograph was taken just outside of a cigar factory on the corner of Gramby and Wolf Streets. The gentleman on the right is Jacob O. Gantz, who raised ponies and ran a haulage company. Loercher Brewery is in the background at left (see page 53). (MHS.)

In this view looking at North Charlotte Street, on the left is the location of Henry Stiegel's store room. This building is said to have been erected around 1875, but it is unknown if or how much of the original structure is shown here. It is still standing but has undergone a number of modifications. Beyond it are, from left to right, the Stroh home (built around 1875), the Gladfelter home (built around 1920), the Double home (built around 1875), and an old log house, which was the first house of worship in Manheim and later a school. (Denny Enck.)

The *Manheim Sentinel* evolved from John M. Ensminger's first newspaper (see page 26). After Ensminger's death in 1899, his print shop continued on as the Sentinel Printing Office, which was built in 1885 on Prussian Street, as shown here. This building was torn down in 1964; however, the structure that was attached to the left of it is still there and is directly across the street from the post office. (MHS.)

A small group of employees are sewing stockings at Samuel Long's stocking factory, which was on the corner of East Gramby and North Wolf Streets. In the 1880s, Long's cigar factory at this location burned to the ground, and he rebuilt it as a stocking factory. (MHS.)

In this late 1800s photograph, George Druckenmiller stands in the doorway of his grocery store on South Prussian Street, near where the fire station is today. The Druckenmillers were one of the founding families of the original Lutheran congregation in Manheim. They are mentioned as one of the first immigrant families in the poem "Stiegel's Schtadt" by Cora Grumling. *Schtadt* is the Pennsylvania Dutch word for "city." (MHS.)

This is the interior of Grace Lutheran Church on South Charlotte Street. It served as a church from 1892 until 1913—first as Grace Lutheran and then as a Methodist congregation. After this time, it was briefly used as the high school, then purchased by A.K. Kauffman, who turned it into the Auditorium Theatre (see page 97). (MHS.)

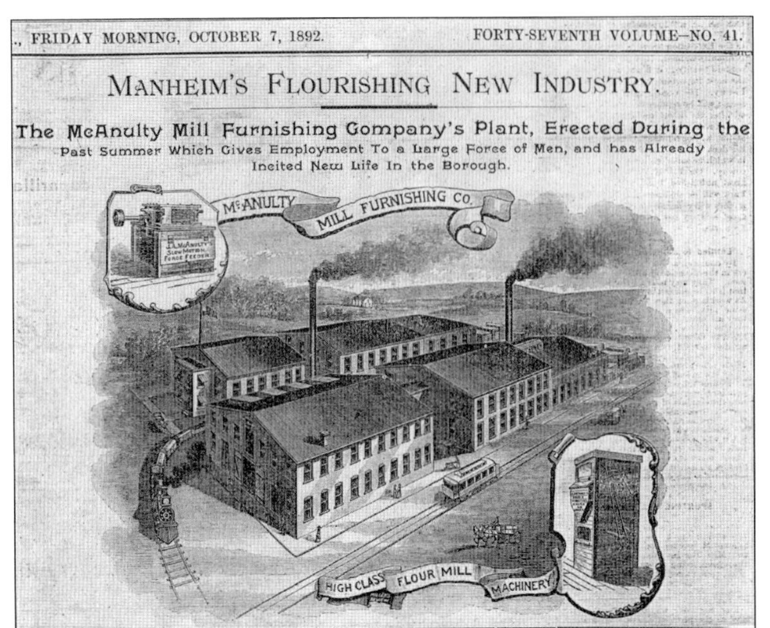

In 1892, McAnulty Mill Furnishing Company was founded in Manheim in what used to be the Manheim Planing Mill. The company designed and built mill machines and supplies. This advertisement shows a large factory conveniently located next to the trolley lines and railroad on the corner of Cherry Street and Railroad Avenue. (MHS.)

This German Baptist church was located on East High Street from 1892 (or 1893) until 1949. The German Baptists were a Christian sect that began 300 years ago in Schwarzenau, Germany. They are also called German Baptist Brethren, Fraternity of German Baptists, Dunkers, and Dunkards. A new church was built in this location, facing Linden Street, in 1949. (MHS.)

A large camp meeting was held in Eby's woods and Kauffman Park in the 1890s. A camp meeting is an outdoor Protestant revival event at which many people pitch tents in a camp and come together to worship, sing, pray, and perform other religious ceremonies. This meeting had over 100 tents, and it was estimated that over 15,000 people had attended on the last day. The largest camp meeting in Manheim was the National Methodist Camp Meeting in 1868, which was held across from Hernley's Mennonite Meeting House. That event hosted an estimated 25,000 people. (Both, MHS.)

From 1893 until 1917, J.C. Shelly ran the People's Restaurant on South Charlotte Street near the railroad station. Note the separate "Ladies Dining Room" door. In those days, some restaurants operated separate dining rooms for women in order to give them a more reputable, segregated space to dine out, as it was not fashionable or respectable for women to visit restaurants, especially if they were alone without a male escort . (MHS.)

George D.C. Danner (left), son of Aaron Danner, and J.H. Sieling (right) show off the hoard of rabbits they caught during a hunt around 1900. Sieling was the initiator of the Festival of the Red Rose at Zion Lutheran Church (see page 21). In 1913, Danner became vice president of the Board of Park Commissioners. (MHS.)

In the fall of 1896, a big storm blew through Manheim, causing damage. This photograph shows a tree that fell down in front of 63 South Main Street. The house did not suffer permanent damage, though, and the Italianate building still stands today (although it has undergone alterations to the first floor to make it a storefront). (MHS.)

In this c. 1900 photograph, a happy group of boys in a tiny carriage are being pulled down the cobblestone streets of Manheim by goats owned by ? Trego. Trego was a horse trainer at the Manheim race track, which opened in 1886. (MHS.)

Manheim's Germania Band is shown here in front of the Prussian House. Although some records state that the Germania Band was founded in 1903 by William E. Longabach, there is a newspaper article about the band performing in 1895 (see page 52). The Chas. V. Wacker & Bro. brewery, noted on the sign, operated from 1884 until 1920, which was when Prohibition started. (MHS.)

In the early 1900s, a large Italianate brick building replaced the Washington House on the corner of Market Square, and it opened as the Washington House Hotel (see page 52). In 1919, in celebration of the end of World War I, a banquet was held here after a memorial service at the Auditorium Theatre. Later, Vogel's clothing store came to this location. (MHS.)

This oxcart was driven by a member of the Becker family and was regularly used at the Mount Hope Grubb estate. On the cart are, from left to right, Charles P. Gibble, Oscar Fisher, John N. Becker, and John G. Graybill. At the time of this 1905 photograph, John Becker owned the store on the right; the structure was later known as the Arndt Building (see page 33). (MHS.)

This home at 101 South Grant Street was built around 1910 and was, for a short period of time, the home of John E. and Fannie Koch and their family. By 1912, it was owned by the Lemans, and the Kochs built a new wood-framed house next door. In 1900, John Koch and Ben Hershey started the Manheim Casting Company, which changed names to the Hershey Machine and Foundry Company in 1906. (MHS.)

Charles Bond established the successful Charles Bond Company in Philadelphia, and it became the city's largest mill supply. In 1905, Bond came to Manheim to begin his new manufacturing company, the Bond Foundry and Machine Company. Although the metal casting foundry burned down in 1974, the factory is still in operation. Today, it is known as Bond Casters and Wheels. The above photograph was taken around 1943. Henry Way, M. Gebert, and Clint Ulrich are shown in the c. 1912 photograph at left. (Both, MHS.)

This snowy scene features another Manheim cigar manufacturer. The sign above the door states, "E.W. Diehm Cigar Manufacturer No. 968 and Dealer in Leaf Tobacco." Cigar factories were given numbers in the 19th century through tax laws. (MHS.)

A livery is a stable where horses are kept and cared for and rented out. Busser's Livery on Prussian Street also manufactured buggies and carriages. The company offered transportation around town and regularly met trains coming in at the railroad station. Busser's Livery also had a contract with the post office to deliver mailbags to and from the railroad station. (MHS.)

The Manheim Fire Department was organized in 1812, and throughout the years, several buildings were used as firehouses. In 1904, the Hope No. 1 firehouse was built on 26 East High Street. The facade above the front door originally read, "1812 Hope No. 1 1904." (Photograph by the author.)

This picture is from the 1904 dedication ceremony for the new Hope No. 1 firehouse. Throughout Manheim's history, a few different fire companies have formed and disbanded, leading to the current firehouse, which was established in 1969—Hope Fire Co. No. 1, located on the corner of South Main and East Ferdinand Streets. (MHS.)

This is an advertisement sheet from sometime between 1900 and 1906. Several names discussed in this book appear on the sheet, which also shows the variety of businesses that flourished in Manheim. Note that there are three cigar manufacturers on this one page alone. Manufacturing cigars was a huge business in Manheim. (MHS.)

In 1906, Horace H. Martin bought the A. Kline Hardware & Lumber Company located at 202 South Charlotte Street. Martin remodeled the building and changed the name to Martin's Hardware Store. This building was replaced in 1946. (MHS.)

In 1906, the US Asbestos Company began operating with only four employees in an abandoned canning factory. It became the largest manufacturing plant in Manheim as it grew to 200 employees by 1914 and 1,400 employees by 1962. In 1929, it became a division of Raybestos-Manhattan, Inc. The plant made the aluminized asbestos metallic cloth heat shielding for NASA's Saturn 1B boosters and firefighting textiles for the US Navy. It also made a wide variety of other products such as Teflon sheets, hoses, and air compressors. In the 1930s, the company started to downplay and conceal the health hazards of asbestos. In 1971, asbestos was classified as a hazardous air pollutant by the Environmental Protection Agency. The company abandoned asbestos and changed its name to Raymark in 1982 but eventually went out of business. (Both, MHS.)

In 1907, Reverend Cooper of the Zion Lutheran Church helped to construct the new parsonage across the street from the church and school. This new brick home and its 1840 neighbor (shown here on the left) are still beautiful houses along High Street today. Reverend Cooper also helped to organize the Manheim Athletic Association in 1911. (MHS.)

Horace Cassel (1885–1949) operated this restaurant on Railroad Avenue. His father, Milton Cassel, bought the property in 1907. Milton owned Fairland Dairy; the dairy's delivery carriage is parked in front of the restaurant in this photograph. In addition to milk, Fairland Dairy also produced ice cream. Milton Cassel also bought Cassel Mill from his father, Henry. (MHS.)

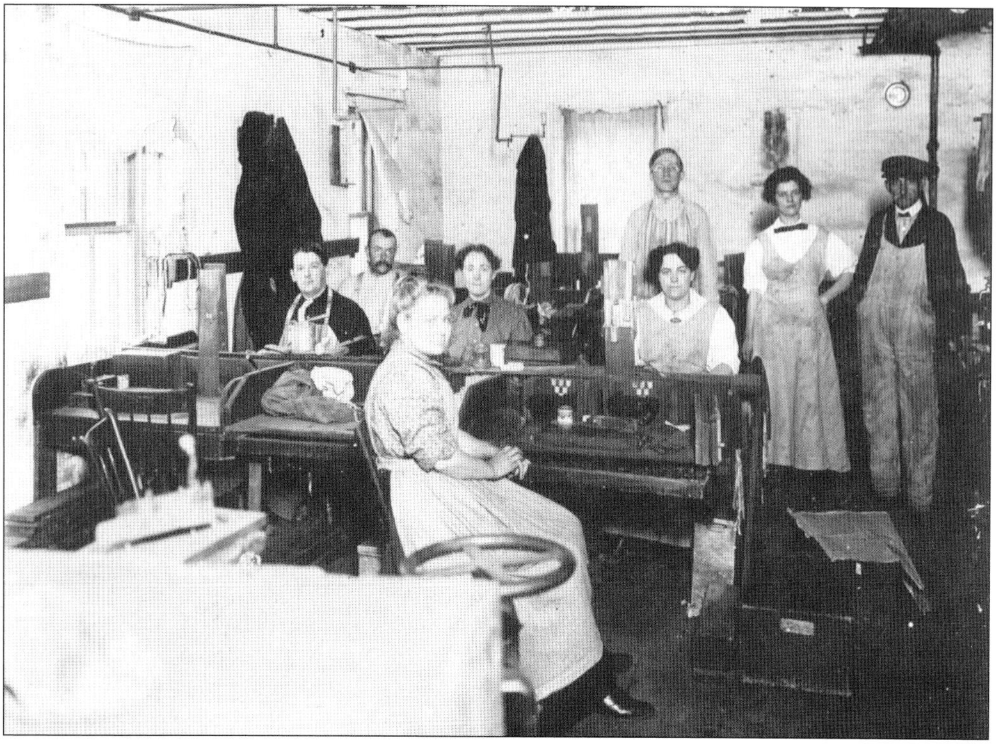

Clayton Gibble, a clothing manufacturer, also started a cigar factory in Manheim. This photograph is from the factory at 27–29 West Gramby Street, a building constructed in the Pennsylvania German Vernacular style. It is still standing. In the photograph are, from left to right, (first row, foreground) unidentified; (second row) Draper Hershey, unidentified (possibly a Mr. Witmyer), Tillie Aston, and Sadie Hershey (Mrs. Draper); (third row, standing) unidentified (possibly Roy Hunchberger), Lizzie Bissinger Frey, and Will Reif. (MHS.)

Henry Stiegel's office was torn down at this location in 1910, and Clayton Gibble, a cigar manufacturer, built an impressive Georgian Revival home here, which is still standing. It is a large two-and-a-half-story yellow brick house with a hipped pyramidal roof and fluted columns on the front portico. The unusually grand building cannot be missed when visiting the square. (Photograph by the author.)

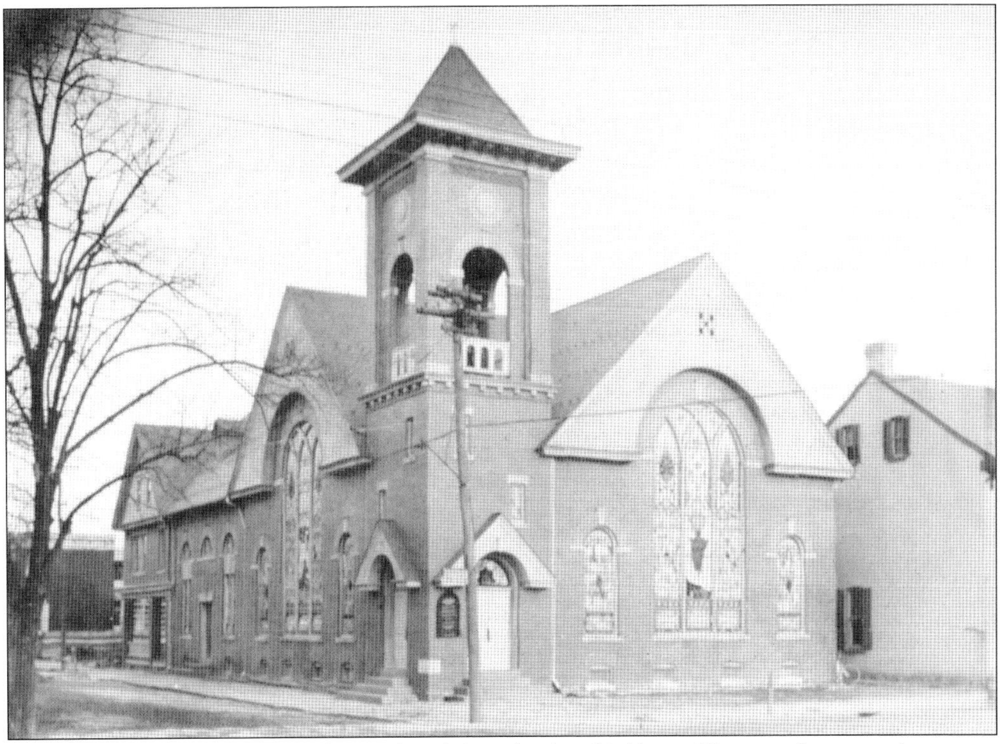

In 1910, the Salem United Brethren Church bought the old Abram Kline residence on the corner of High and Main Streets (see page 54). The congregation razed the building and constructed a new brick church in its place. The Evangelical United Brethren denomination began in 1767 in the United States, and the Manheim congregation formed in 1799. This church was demolished and became a small park in the 1980s. (MHS.)

The original school building on High Street and Hazel Street was torn down, and the new Manheim Public School was constructed in 1914. South Hazel Street is visible next to the school on the right. The building is no longer a school, but it is still standing. (MHS.)

Some current residents may be surprised to know that Manheim was once home to the Opera House at 112 North Main Street. Originally, the building was used for the United Brethren Church. It is not entirely certain where the remains in the cemetery went, but it is thought that many were moved to a different burial ground. The above photograph was taken around 1910 and shows an advertising backdrop on the stage; it includes businesses like the American House, the Summy House, and Litzenberger Hardware. The photograph at left is a fun and charming picture of the Thespian Devils, who performed at the Opera House. From left to right are (first row) Ralph Summy; (second row) Floyd Vogel, Harry Singer, unidentified, and Robert Eberly. (Both, MHS.)

This image shows a performance of the play *Nathan Hale* in approximately 1908 at the Opera House on Prussian Street. Nathan Hale was an American soldier and spy in the Revolutionary War. This play was directed by A.K. Kauffman, who also performed the leading role. After the Opera House closed, the building was taken over by a cigar manufacturer, Eisenlohr Cigar Factory, before the factory moved to the corner of West High and Grant Streets. (MHS.)

Another of Manheim's large manufacturing companies resided on Railroad Avenue. Manheim Knitting Mills was owned by Amos K. Kaufman and produced knit underwear. In addition to owning the Auditorium Theatre and this factory, Kauffman was also president of the Manheim Fire Company in 1912. (MHS.)

The above photograph shows Jefferson Keiffer in his bicycle shop at 108 South Main Street. According to the Lancaster County Historic Resources Inventory, the original building from 1760 is still standing, although it currently looks quite different. At left, Jefferson Keiffer stands with Miles Keiffer (grandson, left) and Frank Keiffer (son or grandson, right). Miles Keiffer became an electrical contractor and an important advocate for Manheim's history. In 1957, Mannheim, Germany, Manheim's namesake, celebrated its 350th anniversary, and to help celebrate, there was a cultural collaboration between the two sister towns called the Town Affiliation Project. Miles Keiffer served as chairman of the committee that helped organize this event. Additionally, he sent some of his own Manheim antique collection to Mannheim for display. In 1962, Keiffer designed the Manheim Borough flag, which was also sent to Mannheim, Germany. (Both, MHS.)

In this charming photograph from the early 20th century (possibly taken during the 1912 Old Home Week), the buggy is being driven by Prof. B.F. Heiges, Helen Becker, and Leona Gingrich on South Grant Street. Today, Grant Street does not have the fields seen here, although it is still quaint. Grant Street was developed from an open dirt road to a built-up town street. (MHS.)

This photograph of the Keystone Hotel was taken in 1912, the same year F.A. Rieker's Brewing Co. (advertised on the sign) was established. Rieker's succumbed to Prohibition in 1920. From 1888 to 1920, the hotel was owned by several people, and M.K. Hoke later opened a store here. The building is still standing on Main Street, and although the front porch and window shutters are gone, one can still recognize it today. (MHS.)

This photograph of the former home of Dr. James M. Dunlap was probably taken after 1912—according to the Manheim Historical Society's records, front porches were built on the homes in the square in that year. This building is still standing in the square today; however, the adjoining neighboring house on the right was removed to make way for the Manheim National Bank's drive-through. Manheim historian John Dunlap Kendig also resided here. (MHS.)

This photograph shows a blacksmith shop on the corner of North Charlotte and West Gramby Streets. Originally, it was "Spondy" Eby's shop and then later became Sam Reed's blacksmith shop. In 1912, there were seven blacksmiths operating in Manheim. (MHS.)

Two rows of seamstresses are shown sewing pantaloons at the Kirchbaum factory on the corner of South Wolf and East Ferdinand Streets. (MHS.)

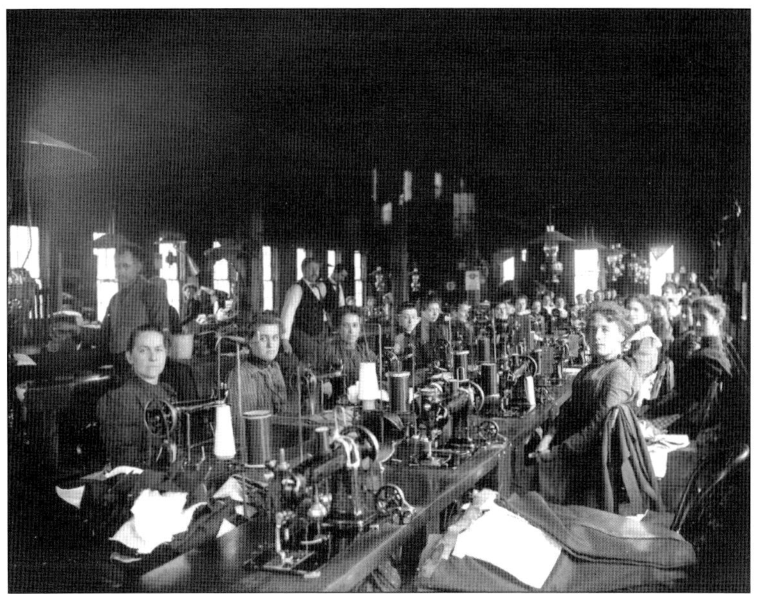

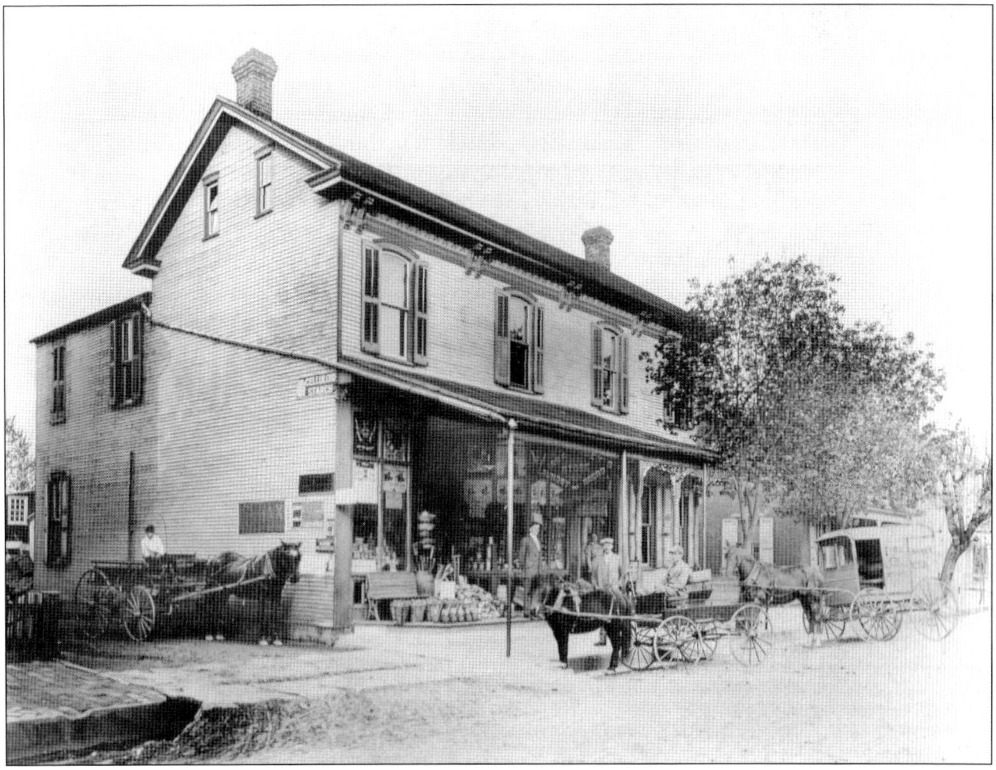

Ira A. Brosey's store sold groceries, phonographs, Graphophones, and bicycles and also offered laundry services. Brosey was heavily involved in the community. For the 1912 Old Home Week celebration, he not only presented a float in the parade but was also the bugler for the decorated automobile caravan that went through 33 towns, drawing attention to the folks pinning up advertisements for the event. In 1921, he served as the first secretary of the County Fireman's Association. (MHS.)

The *Manheim Sentinel* newspaper proudly boasted that the Old Home Week celebration of 1912 was going to be one of the greatest shows not to be missed. On April 12, 1912, the paper extolled, "and now, one and all, get in line and mark time for as sure as shootin', if you do not and are in the way, the steam roller of this Manheim Forward Movement will roll over you and make you feel as flat as one of Mother's good old pan cakes." Many businesses participated in the Industrial Day parade held on July 3, 1912, during the Old Home Week celebration—one of three parades that week. The above photograph shows the Hummer Brothers' contracting company float. Below is a horse-drawn float representing H.H. Martin Lumber/Hardware and Keen Kutter. (Both, MHS.)

This folding fan doubles as an advertisement for Mosemann's Grocery, which was located on Market Square in the original Keystone National Bank building (see page 55). Note the three-digit phone number. (Photograph by the author.)

A group of dapper-looking men is shown riding in a four-horse carriage along the southeast side of Market Square. The buildings are, from left to right, the old Keystone Bank, Graybill's house, and Monroe Pfautz's house. Pfautz built his Georgian Revival house here in 1902 and became burgess of Manheim in 1914. (MHS.)

This picture shows a troop of World War I soldiers in front of the Eisenlohr Cigar Factory on the corner of West High and South Grant Streets. The factory was built in 1912 and began production of hand-rolled Cinco cigars in 1913. William R. Noggle Garment Company bought the factory in 1923. It is currently Graybill's Tool and Die, Inc., a manufacturing company that bought the building in 1977. (MHS.)

A cavalcade of men on horseback trudge through South Main Street, tramping down the deep snow. The two brick houses in the center still remain, although they now have modern storefronts on the first floor. The building at far right has been removed, and that area is now a parking lot in front of Sloan's Pharmacy (see page 45). (MHS.)

The block within the confines of South Hazel, East Mill, South Wolf, and East Ferdinand Streets was originally a field bought by the Manheim Athletic Association in 1912. The organization set up a baseball diamond and park there. In 1919, it was sold to the William R. Noggle Garment Company, which originally resided in the factory on the right in this c. 1929 photograph. Evangelist services and the Manheim Auto Show were once hosted at the building on the left, but it no longer exists. (MHS.)

The William R. Noggle Garment Company had its original factory at 27 East Ferdinand Street. In 1923, it moved to 147 West High Street, which is now home to Graybill's Tool and Die, Inc. Noggle became a member of the first board of directors for the Stiegel Building and Loan Company in 1926. (MHS.)

Chartered in 1865 with capital of $100,000, Manheim National Bank opened its doors at this location. It moved to South Main Street in 1866. In 1924, the bank moved back to this location but in a brand-new Neoclassical building that is still standing today. Manheim National Bank was one of the oldest national banks in Lancaster County. Its presidents included A. Kauffman, H.C. Boyd, and J.L. Graybill. (Photograph by the author.)

The Keystone National Bank was established in 1887 with capital of $60,000. Its presidents included Aaron H. Danner, J.B. Shenk, and J.B. Diehm. In 1925, this hefty gray stone building replaced the home originally located on this corner of Market Square (see page 40). It features tall windows with rounded tops and pillars with acanthus leaf capitals. Its entablature has carved reliefs that show a Beaux-Arts influence—an architectural style that blended French Neoclassicism with Gothic and Renaissance aesthetics. (Photograph by the author.)

This photograph shows the front of John B. Shelly's Restaurant on Railroad Avenue in Manheim. Those pictured are, from left to right, Henry Stormfeltz, Frank White, Aaron Keener, Grant Zook, John Shelly, three unidentified people (on the bench), Dan Heagy, Clayton Shelly, B. Wittle, and Milt Kern. In 1925, three slot machines installed in the restaurant were confiscated by the police; the slot machines had been used primarily by school-aged boys. (MHS.)

The Conestoga Traction Company ran a trolley that traveled between Manheim and Lancaster from 1901 until 1932, when the company introduced a bus service to replace the line. The trolley waiting room is behind the trolley in this view of Main Street looking north. The building at far right (with the arched windows) was the old Pennsylvania Power & Light electric substation, which was later bought by the Lions Club and was eventually torn down. (MHS.)

The first high school in Manheim was established in 1884, the same year water pipes were laid under the streets and the rail line was completed from Manheim to Lebanon. It was not long before the building used for the high school could no longer support the number of enrolled students. In 1926, the first new building dedicated as a high school was opened. It is shown above on the corner of Gramby and Hazel Streets. Despite additions in 1936 and 1952, this building also could not accommodate the increasing volume of students. In 1959, a new Manheim Central High School (below) opened, and it continues to serve the community today. (Both, MHS.)

This photograph from the 1920s or 1930s shows a large group of workers at Andy Metzger's quarry. The quarry has an outcropping that looks a bit like a face. Legend has it that a Native American named Uwagi wanted to live forever in the area. At the moment of his death, he fought against the Great Spirit trying to take him and was struck by lightning, which trapped his likeness in the rock cliff. (MHS.)

From at least 1815 onward, Manheim has had a postmaster. In 1831, a mail line ran from Lancaster to Lebanon via Manheim. Routes and services slowly expanded over the years. By 1920, Manheim had a permanent city delivery route established. In 1935, the US Treasury Department constructed this building—the current post office—on the site of the former home of Aaron Danner, who was the brother of George H. Danner and a president of Keystone National Bank. (MHS.)

These three young acrobats pose in an impressive display in front of the old high school on North Hazel Street. This 1933 photograph shows Donald Saylor, Clair Nissley, and Jean Saylor. Jean Saylor, perched at the top, was nine years old. The plaque on the boulder is a memorial to some of Manheim's fallen soldiers, presented by the Ammon K. Gibble American Legion Post No. 0419. (MHS.)

A.K. Kauffman directed this troupe of Roman ladder performers. Pictured here are, from top to bottom, (left) Christ Royer, Stanley Beamesderfer, Urban Blecher, and Harry Boyd; (center) William Marks, Walter Hoffman, George McCauley, and Lyman Hershey; (right) Jerome Hoffer, Jess Gingrich, Howard Kline, and Louis Kline. (MHS.)

Zion Lutheran Church was adorned with these beautiful decorations for the Festival of the Red Rose (see page 21). The church and its commitment of giving a red rose to Henry Stiegel's descendants was commemorated in Mary Robinson's poem *Ancient Manheim*. Verse two of the poem reads: "She [Manheim] bids all look with rev'rence / Where Stiegel's Zion stands / And, for one red rose payment / Gave of his own broad lands." (MHS.)

In 1934, a group of Baron Stiegel's descendants gathered to celebrate the Festival of the Red Rose. Zion Lutheran Church is in the background, and the family is standing in the cemetery that lies beside it. The Festival of the Red Rose is a tradition that is still celebrated today. (MHS.)

The Festival of the Red Rose has always been a point of pride for the Zion Lutheran Church congregation, and it brings in many guests from near and far. Here, John Stuchell Fisher, who served as a state senator of Pennsylvania from 1901 until 1907 and governor from 1927 until 1931, is attending the festival. (MHS.)

The square in Manheim has undergone many changes in the more than 250 years since it was first plotted. Originally, the square was basically a field that was used not only for traffic but also for celebrations and children's sports, such as baseball. Later additions included pavement, a flagpole, and metered parking. Today, the center median contains trees, flower beds, and a gazebo along with the flagpole that doubles as the center support for a square-wide Christmas light display. (MHS.)

This organ, made by J.B. Henry, has moved around quite a bit. It was originally located in Sheeler's candy store on South Charlotte Street but was later moved to a Lutheran church. Eventually, it was donated to the Hershey Story Museum by John Gish. (MHS.)

In 1936, the Sawdust Warehouse on the corner of Eby and Charlotte Streets caught fire, and the whole factory and one of the neighboring houses burned to the ground. Paul Z. Knier, a member of the Manheim Fire Company and fire marshal of Lancaster County, said that this was one of the most "spectacular" fires he had ever witnessed. (Thomas J. Brendel.)

Creeks and rivers are significant resources for a town, but they can also be a major cause of damage in bad weather. Floods are a regular occurrence in Manheim, with numerous flood events over the years being quite large. The above photograph shows Main Street (looking south) becoming a waterway in 1935. The below photograph shows a flood in 1942. Other notable floods occurred in 1905, 1908, 1969, and 1972, among other years. (Both, MHS.)

This picture shows the Auditorium Theatre with the marquee announcing the black-and-white 1943 movie *What a Woman!* This building was originally constructed in 1892 as Grace Lutheran Church (see page 63). An addition was made to the back of the building in 1913 by Amos K. Kauffman, who then turned it into the Auditorium Theatre. A memorial for Manheim's World War I soldiers was held here the night before the celebrations of Welcome Home Day on October 18, 1919. The theater shut down in the 1970s. (MHS.)

This 1943 aerial photograph shows an athletic field that was given to the borough by the Manheim Athletic Association. The original clay courts and a baseball diamond, both created in 1919, are visible here. This area later became Manheim Veterans Memorial Park and now contains baseball diamonds, a football field, several tennis courts, two basketball courts, and a playground. (MHS.)

These scrap metal piles were a common sight during World War II as communities across the country came together to help fortify the US Army with extra construction materials. In addition to collecting metal, the government also held rubber collection drives, as rubber was another valuable commodity for use in military manufacturing. The whole community became involved in these collections, including women and children. Sometimes the metal donated was not actually scrap metal but instead pots and pans, toys, and fences. In some places, a bust of Hitler was erected so that people could throw their donations at it. These photographs show the scrap pile in Manheim's Market Square. The above view is facing north, and the one below faces south toward the Keystone National Bank (now Fulton Bank). (Both, MHS.)

After World War
II ended, Manheim
honored the men and
women in the armed
forces with a "welcome
home" celebration.
The Manheim Honor
Roll plaque was erected
beside the Keystone
National Bank with a
plaque containing 988
names. Twenty-five of
them were marked with
a gold star, indicating
that they had died in
battle. Today, a different
memorial plaque is
installed there honoring
all of Manheim's
veterans. (MHS.)

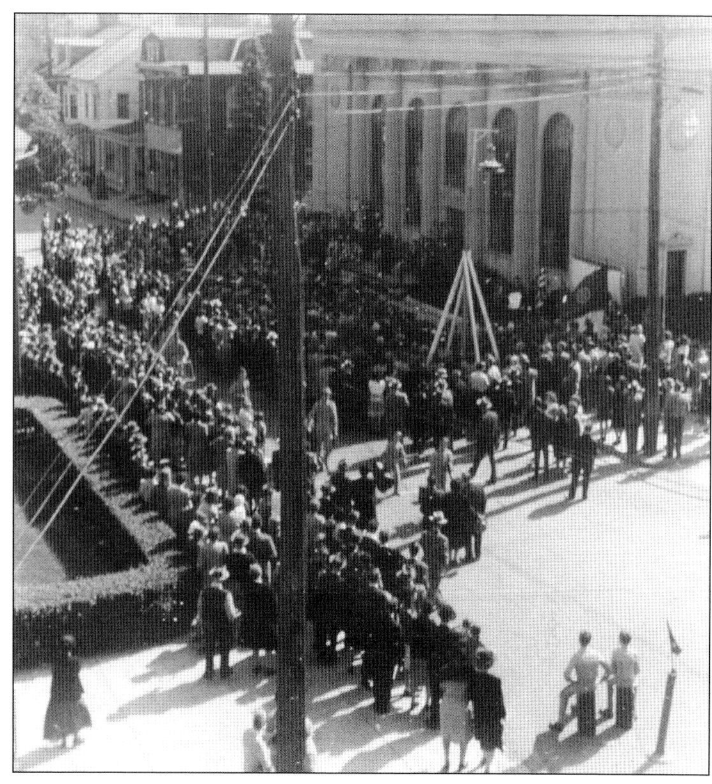

Constructed in the Queen
Anne style in 1880,
this building on South
Main Street is still quite
noticeable, as the round
turret is not a common
architectural feature in
town. Evan's Restaurant
had two other previous
locations in town before
it moved here in 1945. In
1977, it became the Baron
Stiegel Restaurant. The
building no longer houses
a restaurant. (MHS.)

This is a 1949 aerial view that covers an area from nearly the center of town toward the northeast along High Street/Doe Run Road. The sports fields in the upper center later became Manheim Veterans Memorial Park, and the high school was built just to the left of it. Zion Lutheran Church is in the lower right corner. (MHS.)

Charles G. Longenecker bought an existing hardware store on Market Square in 1937 (see page 46). The store shown here was so successful that it outgrew its location. In 1972, a new store—three times bigger—was built on the outskirts of town on Doe Run Road, where it remains in operation today. (MHS.)

Rich Middleton is shown demonstrating a replica of a common press. Sometimes this type of press is called a Franklin press since it was used by Benjamin Franklin, but there were not many design changes made to the printing press between 1450, when it was first invented, and 1780. This replica was made at Manheim Pattern Works at 142 South Pitt Street. (MHS.)

This corner of town was used for manufacturing for a large portion of Manheim's history. This photograph shows the Fuller Company, which took over the Hershey Machine and Foundry Company in 1946 (see page 69). It is currently the property of FLSmidth, Inc., which merged with the Fuller Company in 2001. (MHS.)

George Leonard Heiges (1894–1990), who is posing here with the original indenture document of Charles and Alexander Stedman and Henry William Stiegel, was an important figure in Manheim's history. His multiple ambitious endeavors include but are not limited to being a drugstore owner in Manheim, the supervising principal of Manheim public schools, commander of the American Legion Post No. 0419, and a prolific author of local history, including a book titled *Henry William Stiegel and His Associates* that was published in 1948. (MHS.)

Mrs. Dannehower, wife of Gilbert L. Dannehower, a sixth-generation descendent of Henry William Stiegel, received a single red rose from Zion Lutheran Church in 1953 (see page 21). The rose was presented by Boyd Lee Spahr. In the center is George L. Heiges, chairman of the Rose Service Committee. (MHS.)

Three

AROUND MANHEIM

Surrounding the borough of Manheim are several small villages that are a part of Manheim in both vicinity and mailing addresses. These include the neighborhoods of Mastersonville, Union Square, Sporting Hill, Lancaster Junction, Penryn, White Oak, and Mount Hope. While it is impossible for the scope of this book to fully explore the history of this expansive land, a brief introduction is essential to understanding the breadth of Manheim's culture. These are old villages in Rapho and Penn Townships, which surround the borough. Public highways through the area date back to at least 1702.

The area that would become the village of Mastersonville was settled before the founding of Manheim. Mastersonville lies outside of the borough and can be found by following Colebrook Road northwest out of town. According to the Brubaker genealogy published in the *Mount Joy Bulletin* in 1912, records show that the author's seventh great-grandfather Hans (John) Brubaker, an immigrant from Switzerland, purchased land in this area between 1743 and 1754. It was then known as Grenage/Greenwich. Mastersonville was named after Thomas Masterson, a Catholic immigrant who came from Cavan, Ireland, sometime between 1795 and 1802. He married a German Baptist Brethren girl named Barbara Eshelman. This was a romantic and unique union, as this sort of interreligious marriage was not common in those days. Through his business sense and hard work, Masterson became a wealthy and prominent member of the community, eventually becoming the postmaster.

Sporting Hill can be found by going west on High Street away from town as the road changes into Mount Joy Road. This main road was formerly known as Tulpehocken/Anderson Ferry Road. The village of Sporting Hill was founded in 1800 by David Cassel and was, for some time, called Cassel Town (or Casseltown). It came to be called Sporting Hill due to a couple of "old sports" who frequented the hotel in the village, which was built in 1784.

Peter Grubb purchased land in Mount Hope in 1779, and he built an estate and iron furnace there. Newport Road, one of the oldest and most important roads in the area, led to the furnace and runs through Penryn, White Oak, and what was once Unionville.

Since the beginning of its settlement, Manheim has had a deep connection with agriculture. Its fertile fields were home to the early pioneers, who were predominantly farmers. The farmers surrounding the town used Manheim as a trading and commerce center. Today, the quaint town of Manheim is still surrounded on all sides by rolling green fields dotted with Mennonite, Amish, and modern secular farms. (MHS.)

Shown here is Shenck's Mill on Shenck's Road just outside of Manheim Borough. The covered bridge in the background was built in 1855. It spans Big Chiques Creek and is the third-oldest Lancaster County bridge still open to vehicles. The original farmhouse is still standing, but the orientation does not seem to match the one shown here, so perhaps it was moved (a feat of construction that is not uncommon). (MHS.)

This barn is a classic example of farm architecture in Lancaster County. Rural Manheim is infused with rich farmland that is often owned and operated by Amish and Mennonite families. This photograph was taken by the American Institute of Architects in 1941 for the Pennsylvania German Barn project. (Library of Congress, Prints & Photographs Division, HABS, HABS PA, 36-MAN.V, 1A-1.)

The steam-powered threshing rigs of the late 1800s and early 1900s were expensive, but for those farmers who could afford them, they greatly increased production. This one was owned by Amos T. Frey. From left to right are Amos Snyder, Arthur G. Frey, unidentified, John Henny, unidentified, Amos Frey, unidentified, Herman Ellinger, Emmanuel Fry, and unidentified. (MHS.)

Here is a beautiful example of early barn brickwork. This 1816 barn is located on Wisgarver Road in Mastersonville. The Pennsylvania open-brick style of design is found mainly in the southern part of the state. (Photograph by the author.)

A small Native American graveyard is located just outside of town, heading northeast on Doe Run Road, beside the Kreider Farms buildings. The area around the Chiquesalunga (meaning "place of the crawfish") Creek was home to a few different Native American tribes, including the Conoy, Shawnee, Gawawese, Susquehannock-Conestoga, and Shecassalunga (see page 17). (MHS.)

This lime kiln was built in 1858 just north of town by H.H. and J.H. Hernley. Later, the Gantz family took over this kiln and ran it for three generations. Harry Gantz worked in the kiln for 40 years until he shut it down in 1955. (MHS.)

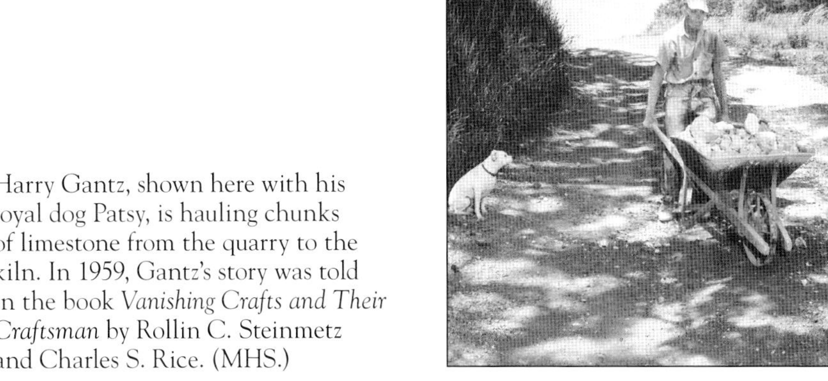

Harry Gantz, shown here with his loyal dog Patsy, is hauling chunks of limestone from the quarry to the kiln. In 1959, Gantz's story was told in the book *Vanishing Crafts and Their Craftsman* by Rollin C. Steinmetz and Charles S. Rice. (MHS.)

Located in the northern Manheim countryside, the Mount Hope estate has a long and interesting history. Unfortunately, the records of the estate's exact history are conflicting, but it appears the land was originally purchased in 1779 by Peter Grubb and became the site of an iron furnace in 1784. The original mansion (above) was built by Peter's son Henry Bates Grubb sometime between 1800 and 1850. It was renovated into the Victorian style (below) in the late 19th century by Daisy Grubb. Today, it is home of the Mount Hope Winery and is a beautiful destination for wine and history enthusiasts. The estate hosts a variety of theater events throughout the year and is home to the beloved perennial Pennsylvania Renaissance Faire, which evolved from a popular jousting tournament that was held by a Maryland jousting club on the site (see page 125). (Both, MHS.)

The Mount Hope iron furnace was built by Peter Grubb in 1784 and later converted to a hot blast furnace by his son during the Industrial Revolution. The hot blast, a new type of furnace, reduced fuel consumption and worked by blasting hot air into a tall furnace filled with iron oxide, flux, and coke; the molten iron and slag was then removed from the bottom of the structure. This furnace has records of employment for a Henry Stiegel after the date he is often said to have died. (MHS.)

Hope Inn was established in 1812 and run by W.F. Hull. This building is still standing, although the porch has been removed, and can be found along Lebanon Road/Route 72 North at the edge of Rapho Township. (MHS.)

This beautiful farmhouse, which is unoccupied but still standing, was once owned by the author's fourth great-grandfather, Rev. Abraham Gibble (1791–1864; last name alternatively spelled Gibbel). He had inherited the house from father-in-law, Isaac Wenger (1757–1825; last name alternatively spelled Weggner). The local Brethren used this house as place of worship before a religious meetinghouse was built. Abraham Gibble was initiated into the White Oak congregation; twice he was disfellowshipped (for unknown reasons), and twice he was reinstated. The house is located on Chiques Road a short distance from Chiques Church of the Brethren. There is a small family graveyard on the site. On the second floor is a post that local people have called a "prayer pole," which may stem from a religious tradition that originated in Europe. (However, it should be noted that the post may simply be a support for the attic.) (Photograph by the author.)

The above photograph, taken around 1915, shows Garman's blacksmith shop in Mastersonville. The original Mastersonville blacksmith shop run, by ? Shonk, is believed to have been behind the main store (see page 112), and it later moved across the street and was run by Hiram Eby. In 1913, Abe Garman took over the shop. He had worked as blacksmith in Elizabethtown starting in 1906, when he was 15 years old. At the time, blacksmithing was a necessary industry, and the borough of Manheim still had several blacksmith shops. The below photograph shows Hiram Eby and Abe Garman inside of Garman's blacksmith shop; the picture is labeled "from Dick Shelly postcard." (Both, MHS.)

This store on Colebrook Road in Mastersonville was built by Benjamin Masterson, son of Thomas Masterson, in 1865. Roy O. Hess's store opened here in 1923. It remained a valuable convenience store for the community until around 1999 and is now a furniture store. The Mastersonville Volunteer Fire Department was incorporated in 1950, and the department kept their fire engine in Hess's garage behind the store until they could acquire a fire station. (MHS.)

This is the Exchange Hotel in Mastersonville. It was built around 1880 by Samuel R. Zug. Zug was influential in the development of Elizabethtown College in nearby Elizabethtown. The college was chartered in 1899 by members of the Church of the Brethren. (MHS.)

Although this structure has been known by many names throughout history (including Hill Church, which it is still called by some), the congregation of Trinity Evangelical Lutheran Church of Colebrook on Church Road dates back to 1771. In 1772, wardens and trustees from the German Lutheran Congregation bought this property, which already had a church erected on it, from Curtis Grubb. The new church (pictured) was built in 1842 and remains part of the church today, although additions have been made. Some of the graves in the cemetery date to the late 1770s. (MHS.)

This is a picture of the farm of David Cassel (founder of Sporting Hill), which was located at the bottom of Cassel's Hill on Power Road just outside the south end of town (see page 103). Although records could not be found for these buildings, when one compares this photograph to the present site, it appears as though all three of these structures still exist. (MHS.)

The Wenger family's coachworks company in Sporting Hill was first run by Abraham Wenger; his son Amos took over in 1883. In an 1892 article about the coachworks, it was said that Abraham Wenger "was recognized as one of the best coach makers in the county." (MHS.)

Kauffman's Distillery, owned by Henry Kauffman (1821–1894), operated from 1803 to 1890 in Sporting Hill; before that, it was run by Jacob S. Kauffman (1749–1849). The history of the distillery goes back to at least the time of the Revolutionary War. A nearby covered bridge named after this distillery was built on Sun Hill Road in 1857. It was rebuilt in 1874 and is still standing today. (MHS.)

This memorial plaque is located on a large boulder at the intersection of Newport and Gish Roads in Penryn. The memorial explains Matthias Gish's contributions to the area. (MHS.)

The Hoke Hotel was located in Penryn. A fire at the hotel in 1912 became a catalyst for the founding of the Penryn Fire Association. The association's first chemical apparatus was housed in a rented horse stable at the Hoke Hotel. Medicine shows were also performed here; these were entertainments meant to draw in customers who would then be presented with medicines to buy. (MHS.)

This bridge crosses Big Chiques Creek in Lancaster Junction. The land along this creek was once inhabited by the Chicquesaw, a branch of the Conestoga tribe. In 1860, the Reading Company constructed a rail line from Lancaster Junction to Columbia. (Library of Congress, Prints & Photographs Division, HAER, HAER PA-630.)

This photograph shows a group of men dividing and cutting up ice blocks on Keller's Dam. This dam is located in the countryside on the way to White Oak. Ice was stored in a massive icehouse and separated by layers of sawdust. (MHS.)

Four

MANHEIM TODAY

The pride that Manheim residents felt for their community during Old Home Week in 1912 has continued on through generations. In 1957, Manheim and the town of Mannheim in Germany collaborated to celebrate the sisterhood of these two towns across the Atlantic Ocean. As Mannheim celebrated the 350-year anniversary of its founding, the Town Affiliation Project was sponsored by the US Information Agency. Visitors from each town traveled to the other and exchanged gifts and mementos.

Manheim commemorated its bicentennial in 1962 with a book—*Manheim Bicentennial 1762–1962: Our Stiegel Heritage*—that featured Manheim's history, organizations, and community leaders. A large and festive parade sauntered through town as well.

In 1950, the Manheim Central School District was formed and included Manheim Borough, Rapho Township, and Penn Township. Between 1952 and 1995, 30 one-room school buildings were closed down, and their students were distributed to five new elementary schools.

Manheim's long history of printing came to an end, for the most part, in 1967, when the *Manheim Sentinel* went out of business; however, Stiegel Printing, Inc., printed a regular newspaper, *Stiegel News*, from 1967 to 1978.

The current owners of Mount Hope Estate & Winery continue to promote its history, and it makes for a wonderful historic destination. This estate also hosts the Pennsylvania Renaissance Faire, which is a massively successful seasonal festival.

The Manheim Auto Auction was founded in Manheim in 1945. By 1959, it had become the largest auto auction in the world. Over the coming decades, the company grew and established operations in locations all over the world while retaining its original home in Manheim. A 200-acre car lot may not be the most aesthetically appealing thing to accompany this otherwise beautiful country town, but it does provide a large and secure industry for the community.

Manufacturers, unique shops, restaurants, and community events snuggle in together among the many historical buildings. The surrounding farm life continues, often in ways that are not very different than in times past. Manheim breathes small-town charm as it progresses onward through history.

This 1958 picture looks similar to the view today, with street parking in the center of the square and the two large brick buildings being used for commercial purposes. However, the wood-frame buildings on the left have since been replaced with brick structures. (MHS.)

When the community swimming pool opened in 1958, many older residents felt it was not a worthwhile effort, as Chiques Creek had always provided young people with a means for summer swimming. However, the pool was built at the end of Manheim Veterans Memorial Park and continues to be loved in town. It was the first community-sponsored swimming pool in Lancaster County. (MHS.)

In June 1962, Manheim threw a celebration to honor its 200th anniversary. Much of this book's information was collected from a small book published for this celebration called *Manheim Bicentennial 1762–1962: Our Stiegel Heritage*. Collaborating on the book's editorial committee were Loy C. Awkerman, George L. Heiges, and John Dunlap Kendig. The introduction of the book stated that the previous 25 years showed "phenomenal growth" for Manheim. In the photograph at right, a parade is passing in front of the Arndt Building on Main Street, which was then Rettew's Department Store (and the original location of Henry Stiegel's mansion; see page 33). In the below photograph, the Manheim Central High School marching band is strutting through the streets of town. (Both, MHS.)

Floods ripped through Manheim in 1972, when Hurricane Agnes came up the East Coast from the Caribbean. This would go down in history as one of the largest June hurricanes on record. Fifty out of the 122 deaths from the hurricane occurred in Pennsylvania, and it caused $2 billion in damages in the Susquehanna River basin. The above photograph shows a canoe tied to horse posts on East Ferdinand Street. The below photograph was taken on Main Street looking south. Manheim has had frequent floods over the years. The south end of town has always been a problematic flood area. In 1999, several houses were torn down on South Hazel Street, and those properties were turned into Swan Park, a grassy area with a walking trail. (Both, MHS.)

With ornate highlights that would delight even Baron von Stiegel, this classic Manheim Central High School drum majorette uniform is on display at the Manheim Historical Society along with a shiny baton. It was donated by the high school's music department. The majorette who wore this undoubtedly would have marched through town during parades proudly accompanying the rest of her fellow Barons. (Photograph by the author.)

The first community farm show in Manheim took place in 1915. The Manheim Farm Show was organized in 1953 and continues to be a much-loved event in the community. The Manheim Community Farm Show Complex, located beside the high school on Adele Avenue, is a permanent structure dedicated to the show. The show includes displays and events featuring agriculture, animal husbandry, food, and arts and crafts. A farm show parade and children's costume contest parade are also held during the event. (MHS.)

Root's Country Market and Auction began in 1925 as a poultry auction founded by A.W. Root. It is located just outside of the borough on Graystone Road. Through five generations, it has remained a favorite shopping destination for locals. On Tuesdays, customers can purchase produce, baked goods, meat, and live animals. The space is also home to a flea market and an antique market. (Above, Root's Country Market and Auction; below, MHS.)

The Historic Manheim Preservation Foundation Museum & Archives is a small operation on Market Square across from the Danner Building. The foundation was started by Elizabeth Keiffer, who wanted a way to share her and her husband Miles Keiffer's love of Manheim history and the artifacts they had collected over the years (see page 80). The foundation also has a small library, archives, a garden dedicated to Elizabeth, and a carriage house in back that can be used for meetings. (Photograph by the author.)

Stiegel Glassworks 1976 is a small artisan glass company that operates on the property of the Manheim Historical Society beside the Manheim Railroad Station museum. The company practices traditional glass techniques used by Henry Stiegel more than 250 years ago. The "1976" in the company's name is in reference to the US bicentennial, which is when glassblowing was reawakened in Manheim. In addition to the glassworks available at the company's shop and other local retailers, Stiegel Glassworks 1976 also offers educational glassblowing experiences and fulfills custom orders. (Photograph by the author.)

This corner of Main and High Streets has seen a lot of changes over the years. It was originally a residential property that was torn down for the construction of Salem United Brethren Church in 1910 (see pages 54 and 77). In the 1980s, the church was torn down and a small park was built in its place. The trees have grown, but the park still remains, as shown here. (MHS.)

The town clock was purchased by the Manheim Historical Society in 1994 and is located along Main Street beside the small park on the corner of Main and High Streets. It was made by E. Howard & Co. in Boston, Massachusetts, and was first brought to Manheim in 1926 by the Flinchbaugh Jewelry Store. After 136 years, the clock remains in working order. (Photograph by the author.)

Daisy Grubb, who enlarged and remodeled the Mount Hope mansion in the late 19th century, passed away in 1936 and was the last member of the Grubb family to reside at the estate (see page 108). The estate was held by several owners over the years until Chuck Romito bought it in 1979. The following year, he opened the Mount Hope Winery. Romito collaborated with a Maryland jousting club to host jousting tournaments at the estate. The tournaments' popularity grew, and out of that, the Pennsylvania Renaissance Faire was born. Today, the fair is an annual event held on the Mount Hope property and receives over 200,000 guests per year. The much beloved fair still includes jousting tournaments as well as other medieval and Renaissance-style entertainment, games, food, and arts and crafts. (Both, Pennsylvania Renaissance Faire.)

The American House building (see page 37) was remodeled in 1986 and became The Cat's Meow restaurant in 1987. Today, the food and Roaring Twenties atmosphere at The Cat's Meow are still enjoyed by patrons. (Photograph by the author.)

The Harry B. Shearer Heritage Center at 88 South Grant Street is home to the Manheim Historical Society, which was founded in 1964. The heritage center and the society are genuine treasures for the community of Manheim. The heritage center contains artifacts on display, thousands of photographs, a library of local history, and archives of newspapers, deeds, and maps. The historical society also owns historical sites around town, including the Keath and Fasig Houses and the railroad station, which is available for event rental. The society also organizes community events. (Photograph by the author.)

BIBLIOGRAPHY

Awkerman, Loy C., George L. Heiges, and John Dunlap Kendig, eds. *Manheim Bicentennial 1762–1962: Our Stiegel Heritage.* Manheim, PA: Sentinel Printing House, 1962.

Ellis, Franklin, and Samuel Evans. *History of Lancaster County Pennsylvania, with Biographical Sketches of Many of Its Pioneers and Prominent Men.* Philadelphia, PA: Everts & Peck, 1883.

Heiges, George L. *Henry W. Stiegel and His Associates: A Story of Early American Industry.* Manheim, PA: The Arbee Foundation, 1976.

Kashatus, William C. "William Penn's Legacy: Religious and Spiritual Diversity." *Pennsylvania Heritage* Vol. 37, No. 2 (2011).

Lancaster County Historic Resources Inventory. ir.co.lancaster.pa/us/hri/.

"Manheim Borough Historic District," Living Places Neighborhoods. www.livingplaces.com.

Manheim Historical Society. *Manheim Revisited 1700–2000.* Morgantown, PA: Mastof Press, 2000.